Evil Dead
The Musical

High School Version

Book and lyrics by
GEORGE REINBLATT

Music by
FRANK CIPOLLA, CHRISTOPHER BOND,
MELISSA MORRIS and GEORGE REINBLATT

Music supervision by
FRANK CIPOLLA

Additional lyrics by
CHRISTOPHER BOND

Additional music by
ROB DALEMAN

Dramatic Publishing Company
Woodstock, Illinois ● Australia ● New Zealand ● South Africa

*** NOTICE ***

©MMXVII by
Book and lyrics by GEORGE REINBLATT
Music by FRANK CIPOLLA, CHRISTOPHER BOND,
MELISSA MORRIS and GEORGE REINBLATT
Music supervision by FRANK CIPOLLA
Additional lyrics by CHRISTOPHER BOND
Additional music by ROB DALEMAN

Printed in the United States of America
All Rights Reserved
(EVIL DEAD THE MUSICAL [HIGH SCHOOL VERSION])

For inquiries concerning all other rights, please visit:
www.evildeadthemusical.com

ISBN: 978-1-61959-160-8

IMPORTANT BILLING AND CREDIT REQUIREMENTS

All producers of the musical *must* give credit to the bookwriter and composers of the musical in all programs distributed in connection with performances of the musical and in all instances in which the title of the musical appears for purposes of advertising, publicizing or otherwise exploiting the musical and/or a production. The names of the bookwriter and composers *must* also appear on a separate line, on which no other names appear, immediately following the title, and *must* appear in size of type not less than fifty percent (50%) the size of the title type. The special credit requirements following the names of the bookwriter and composers must appear in size of type not less than 25% the size of the names of the bookwriter and composers. Specific credit must read as follows:

EVIL DEAD
THE MUSICAL
Book and lyrics by
George Reinblatt
Music by
Frank Cipolla   Christopher Bond
Melissa Morris   George Reinblatt
Music supervision by
Frank Cipolla
Additional lyrics by
Christopher Bond
Additional music by
Rob Daleman
By special arrangement with
Renaissance Pictures, Ltd. & Studio Canal Image SA
Originally produced in New York by
Jenkay LLC, Jeffrey Latimer Entertainment, Just For Laughs Live
for
Idle Dave Productions LLC

Biographical information on the bookwriter and composers, if included in the playbook, may be used in all programs.

Evil Dead The Musical first glimpsed the light of day in Toronto, where early workshop engagements played to capacity and beyond. While mainstream audiences flocked to the show, diehard *Evil Dead* fans made pilgrimages from across North America to witness the birth of a new cult hit. The popular workshop production enjoyed two sold-out runs at Toronto's Transac Club in 2003 before heading off to Montreal in 2004 as part of the 22nd Just For Laughs Festival.

Evil Dead The Musical opened in New York off-Broadway produced by Jenkay LLC, Jeffrey Latimer Entertainment, Just for Laughs Live, at New World Stages on Nov. 1, 2006. The performance was directed by Christopher Bond and Hinton Battle, with sets by David Gallo, costumes by Cynthia Nordstrom, lighting by Jason Lyons, sound design by Peter Fitzgerald and Kevin Lacy, special effects and makeup design by Louis Zakarian, fight choreograhy by B.H. Barry, choreography by Hinton Battle, sound effects design by Michael Laird. The Production Stage Manager was Jane Pole. The cast was as follows:

LINDA .... Jennifer Byrne
CHERYL .... Jenna Coker
SHELLY .... Renée Klapmeyer
ASH .... Ryan Ward
SCOTT .... Brandon Wardell
ED .... Tom Walker
ANNIE .... Renée Klapmeyer
MOOSE .... Tom Walker
JAKE .... Darryl Winslow
FAKE SHEMP .... Ryan Williams
SPIRIT OF KNOWBY .... BrandonWardell

The band consisted of:
CONDUCTOR/KEYBOARDS .... Daniel Feyer
GUITAR/BANJO .... Jake Schwartz
DRUMS/PERCUSSION .... Brad "Gorilla" Carbone

Evil Dead The Musical (High School Version) premiered at Stagedoor Manor in Loch Sheldrake, New York, in the Jack Romano Playhouse on July 28, 2017. The performance was executive produced by the Samuelson/Samen family, under the guidance of Director of Theatrical Programming Chris Armbrister, directed by Rob Scharlow, musical direction by James Mablin, choreography by Madeline Shaffer, stage management by Hannah Delmore, assistant stage management by William K. Brooks, fight choreography by Chris Armbrister, scenic design by Stephanie Baugher, lighting design by Sarah "Bob" Johnson-Baldwin, costume design by Mary Reed, props by Rob Brown, make-up by Jordayne Whitfield. The Production Stage Manager was Carolyn Hight. The cast was as follows:

ASH.. Kevin Dolan
CHERYL..Briana Fleming
SCOTT... Josh Lee
LINDA .... Amanda Roit
SHELLY.. Andrea Mitchell
ANNIE .... Hailey Rock
JAKE... Samuel Masto
ED .... Andrew Wantula
MOOSE... Charlie Walker
KNOWBY.. James Persons
SPIRITS/DEMONS/CUSTOMERS ....Mullane Andreychuk, Michaela Baxter, Lily Kate Forbes, Ava Foster, Isabella Giannetti, Avery Goodman, Heather Harris, Nicolette Julien, Alexandra Kafrissen, Chloe Oldland, Lily Ryan, Rebecca Smith, Emma Stopek, Reilly Wilmit

Musical Accompaniment:
PIANO..James Mablin

Evil Dead
The Musical
(High School Version)

CHARACTERS

ASH (m): College student, baritone.
CHERYL (w): College student, alto.
ANNIE (w): Mid-20s, alto.
SHELLY (w): College student, alto.
LINDA (w): College student, soprano.
SCOTT (m): College student, tenor.
ED (m): Mid-20s, bass.
MOOSE (m): Cartoon moose voice, bartone/tenor.
JAKE (m): Mid-30s, baritone.
KNOWBY (m): 60-year-old professor, non-singing.

INDIVIDUAL CHORUS ROLES:

AIRPORT ANNOUNCER	POSSESSED WOMAN
CUSTOMER 1	LINDA'S HEADLESS BODY
CUSTOMER 2	BEAVER
CUSTOMER 3	EVIL FORCE
MOM CUSTOMER	SEVERED HAND
FEMALE CUSTOMER	

GROUP CHORUS ROLES:
EVIL TREES
HOUSE SPIRITS
DEMONS
CUSTOMERS

MUSICAL NUMBERS

ACT I

1. Cabin in the Woods 11

2. Housewares Employee 23

*2a. Cheryl vs. the Trees 26

3. It Won't Let Us Leave 29

4. Look Who's Evil Now 33

5. What the Heck Was That 38

6. Join Us 42

*6a. Join Us - Ash Hand Fight 45

7. Good Old Reliable Jake 47

*7a. Look Who's Evil Now (Sting #1) 51

8. Housewares Employee (Reprise) 52

*8a. Look Who's Evil Now (Sting #2) 53

9. I'm Not a Killer 55

*The underscored songs indicated with a letter should not be listed in a program.

ACT II

10. I'm Not a Killer (Reprise).. 57

*10a. Look Who's Evil Now (Sting #3) 61

11. Bit Part Demon.. 62

12. All the Men in My Life Keep Getting

    Killed by Candarian Demons 67

*12a. Look Who's Evil Now (Sting #4) 74

13. Ode to an Accidental Stabbing...................................... 74

*13a. Housewares Employee (Piano Reprise)..................... 77

*13b. Grabbing the Pages Fanfare 78

*13c. Chainsaw Fanfare.. 79

14. Do the Necronomicon... 80

15. It's Time 84

16. We Will Never Die... 87

*16a. Look Who's Evil Now (Sting #5) 89

17. Blew That Witch Away 90

*17a. Bows.. 95

*17b. Exit Music (aka "Groovy").. 95

*The underscored songs indicated with a letter should not be
    listed in a program.

PRODUCTION NOTES

The cast size may be reduced to a minimum of eight performers, or expanded to an unlimited number of performers. Please see the Casting Notes in the back of the book for additional information on how to reduce or expand the cast size.

As this show uses many pop culture references, the author periodically provides updates to the book and lyrics to keep it fresh. These approved updates are available from the publisher.

Also, please see the back of the book for notes and suggestions regarding set design.

Evil Dead
The Musical
(High School Version)

ACT I

Scene 1

(A lone spotlight comes up on a giant Necronomicon. The book opens on its own, as the text, written in blood, fills the page.)

KNOWBY *(V.O.)*. Legend has it that it was written by the Dark Ones. Necronomicon ex Mortis, roughly translated, "Book of the Dead." The book served as a passageway to the evil worlds beyond. It was written long ago, when the seas ran red with blood. It was this blood that was used to ink the book. In the year thirteen hundred A.D., the book disappeared.

(The book slams shut. Lights up on ASH, LINDA, SCOTT, SHELLY and CHERYL in a car.)

(#1: "Cabin in the Woods")

ALL.
> WE'RE ALL JAMMED IN THE CAR
> AND WE'RE GOING REALLY FAR
> DRIVING DEEP INTO THE TREES
> WITH HOT DOGS, CHIPS, AND CHEESE
>
> TO MAKE THE WEEK GO QUICKER
> WE PACKED A CASE OF SNICKERS
> COKE AND TROPICANA
> WE'LL GO TOTALLY BANANAS!

ALL *(cont'd)*.

> SPRING BREAK VACATION IS JUST *BLING BLING*
> 'CAUSE SOMETHING IN THIS MUSTY AIR MAKES
>   US WANT TO SING

> CABIN IN THE WOODS (OOOH)
> A CABIN IN THE WOODS (YEAH)
> WE'RE FIVE COLLEGE STUDENTS ON OUR WAY
>   TO AN OLD ABANDONED CABIN IN THE
>   WOODS (*OOOH YEAH*)

ASH. Well kids, after a three hour drive, I can officially say, we're here.

SHELLY. I don't see any cabin in the woods.

ASH. That's because it's in the woods. The woods just up there. But this is as far as the road goes. In order to get to the cabin, we have to cross this footbridge. *(Points to a small bridge.)* It is the only way to the cabin. The only way.

LINDA. Oh Ash, as much as I love working with you everyday at S-Mart, I think this vacation will be even better.

ASH. I couldn't agree more, Linda. Sometimes it's healthy for a boyfriend and girlfriend to leave their place of employment and just have some fun as a couple, in a non S-Mart related setting.

(LINDA crosses the bridge.)

CHERYL. Thanks for bringing me along, Ash.

ASH. Please, Cheryl. Would it be a spring break vacation if I didn't drag along my lonely sister?

(CHERYL crosses the bridge.)

SHELLY. Hey, Ash, thanks for letting me come on this trip.

ASH. Well, Shelly, if you were good enough for Scott to pick up at a bus stop three days ago, then I just know you're good enough for me to spend my only holiday of the year with.

(SHELLY crosses the bridge.)

SCOTT. This cabin is gonna kick some serious—

ASH *(cutting him off)*. Yes it is, Scotty. Yes, it is.

SCOTT *(to the girls, while crossing bridge)*. Hey, wait for me! Geez!

ASH.
> ALL MY FRIENDS ARE HERE
> FOR THE BEST SPRING BREAK OF THE YEAR
> AWAY FROM SCHOOL AND FROM S-MART
> FOR A WEEK WAY OFF THE CHARTS

LINDA.
> A HOLIDAY WITH ASH
> ALL THAT I'D EVER ASK
> HE'S SO CUTE AND THIN
> AND THAT'S WHY I LOVE HIM

SCOTT.
> THIS WILL BE JUST LIKE CAMP
> AND SHE'S DUMB AS A LAMP
> IN A FEW HOURS YOU WILL SEE ME
> TASTING HER TONSILS IN A TREE

SHELLY.
> SCOTT'S LOOKING TO GET BUSY
> BUT FRESH AIR MAKES ME DIZZY
> I'M SO HIS PERFECT GIRL
> *OH LOOK, THERE GOES A SQUIRREL!*

CHERYL.

> A WEEK UP IN THE WOODS OF PURE
> TRANQUILITY
> A CHANCE FOR ME TO REST IN A NICE FACILITY
> I CAME UP TO THIS CABIN TO READ AND SLEEP
> AND BAKE

SCOTT.

> HOPE OUR ALL-NIGHT PARTIES DON'T KEEP MISS
> BORING AWAKE!

ALL.

> CABIN IN THE WOODS (OOOH)
> A CABIN IN THE WOODS (YEAH)
> WE'RE FIVE COLLEGE STUDENTS ON OUR WAY
> TO AN OLD ABANDONED CABIN IN THE
> WOODS (*OOOH YEAH*)

LINDA. Hey, Ash! What's this place like anyway?

ASH. Well, it's an old place. A little run down, but it's right up in the mountains. And the best part is, we're staying there for free.

LINDA. Yeah, why are we getting this place for free?

CHERYL. What kind of landlord rents cabins for free?

SCOTT. No landlord rents cabins for free. That's why we're not renting it.

LINDA. What?

ASH. Yeah, I forgot to tell you girls. We're not exactly renting this cabin.

SCOTT. We're breaking in.

CHERYL. No!

ASH. Don't worry. No one will find out. At this time of year, the owners won't be there.

SHELLY. You mean, we're breaking into an empty cabin in the woods? I don't like the sounds of this.

SCOTT. What can possibly go wrong with five college students breaking into an abandoned, secluded, cabin in the woods, where no one knows where we are?

SHELLY. Well, when you put it that way!

ASH.
> THIS TRIP WILL BE WACKY FUN

LINDA.
> SEVEN DAYS TO SNUGGLE MY HONEY BUN

SHELLY.
> *A WEEK OF TANNING*

SCOTT.
> AND US GETTIN' BUSY

CHERYL.
> *AND TONIGHT I'LL MAKE SOME SNACKS THAT WILL ALL BE GLUTEN FREE!*

ALL.
> LISTEN TO US NOW AND MAKE NO MISTAKE
> WE'RE GONNA HAVE FUN 'CAUSE IT'S SPRING BREAK
> *WE'LL SCORE, WE'LL SNORE, WE'LL* EAT FOOD OFF THE FLOOR.
> WE'LL DO ALL THIS AND A WHOLE LOT MORE—IN OUR
>
> CABIN IN THE WOODS (OOOH)
> A CABIN IN THE WOODS (YEAH)
> WE'RE FIVE COLLEGE STUDENTS ON OUR WAY TO AN OLD ABANDONED CABIN IN THE WOODS *(YEAH)*

SHELLY.
YEAH

ASH & LINDA.
FIVE COLLEGE
STUDENTS ON
OUR WAY TO AN
OLD ABANDONED
CABIN IN THE
WOODS
CABIN IN THE
WOODS
CABIN IN THE
WOODS

WE'RE FIVE
COLLEGE
STUDENTS ON
OUR WAY TO AN
OLD ABANDONED
CABIN IN THE
WOODS
CABIN IN THE
WOODS
CABIN IN THE
WOODS

WE'RE FIVE
COLLEGE
STUDENTS ON
OUR WAY TO AN
OLD ABANDONED
CABIN IN THE
WOODS
CABIN IN THE
WOODS
CABIN IN THE
WOODS

SCOTT & SHELLY.
WE'RE FIVE
COLLEGE
STUDENTS ON
OUR WAY TO AN
OLD ABANDONED
CABIN IN THE
WOODS
CABIN IN THE
WOODS
CABIN IN THE
WOODS

WE'RE FIVE
COLLEGE
STUDENTS ON
OUR WAY TO AN
OLD ABANDONED
CABIN IN THE
WOODS
CABIN IN THE
WOODS
CABIN IN THE
WOODS

WE'RE FIVE
COLLEGE
STUDENTS ON OUR
WAY TO AN OLD
ABANDONED

CHERYL.
WE'RE FIVE
COLLEGE
STUDENTS ON
OUR WAY TO AN
OLD ABANDONED
CABIN IN THE
WOODS
CABIN IN THE
WOODS
CABIN IN THE
WOODS

WE'RE FIVE
COLLEGE
STUDENTS ON
OUR WAY TO AN
OLD ABANDONED
CABIN IN THE
WOODS
CABIN IN THE
WOODS
CABIN IN THE
WOODS

ALL.
CABIN IN THE WOODS

(Exit all.)

Scene 2

(Inside the cabin. The group enters.)

ASH. So this is our cabin in the woods. Isn't it great?

EVIL FORCE. Join us.

CHERYL. Did you hear something?

SCOTT. No.

(SCOTT runs back to the bedrooms.)

LINDA. Look at this place. Oh, it's fantastic, Ash.

ASH. Sure is, Linda.

SHELLY. Ohhh windows … fancy.

(SCOTT returns.)

SCOTT. Wow. You should see all the bedrooms back there. They're freakin' awesome. I call top bunk.

SHELLY. There's beds here too? Oh la la.

CHERYL. I feel funny about being here. What if the people who own the place come home?

ASH. They're not gonna come back. Even if they do, we'll tell them the car broke down or something like that.

LINDA. With your car, they'd believe it.

SCOTT. Stop worrying, Cheryl. Why don't you go read or something?

CHERYL. Maybe I will.

(CHERYL pulls out Bruce Campbell's book If Chins Could Kill.*)*

SCOTT *(to SHELLY)*. What's her problem?

SHELLY. I know. She thinks she's so smart just 'cause she can read.

ASH. This is the life. All the important people in my life here together. My girlfriend. My sister. My best friend. And of course you, Shelly, who I only just met. But still, I couldn't think of four other people in the world I'd rather spend my vacation with. I would very much like to make a toast for all this evening. *(Holding up a glass.)* As a Greek friend of mine once said, "Oh nis nis tu tu tarine."

LINDA. Which means?

SCOTT. Party down!

(Suddenly, the cellar door flings open on its own.)

ASH. What was that?

LINDA. Whatever it is, it's still down there.

CHERYL. I don't like cellars. Let's just close it up. It's probably just some animal.

SCOTT. An animal? An animal? *(Laughs.)* That is the stupidest thing I've ever heard of. Holy cow. What a stupid jerk.

CHERYL. Well then maybe it was the wind.

SCOTT. The wind? We're inside! I thought what you said before was stupid. But now that is the stupidest thing I've ever heard. What a stupid jerk!

LINDA. There's definitely something down there. And it probably is just some animal. Ash, remember when we had that raccoon in the basement at S-Mart?

ASH. Remember? I had to use a broom, a laundry hamper and a Swiffer just to get rid of it. But don't worry, loyal S-Mart shoppers, we removed the animal and S-Mart was once again rodent-free.

SCOTT. Well, you guys are probably right. Probably is just some animal. Here, Cheryl, why don't you go down 'n check, make sure?

CHERYL. Scotty! I'm not going down there!

SCOTT. Ha ha ha. What a stupid jerk!

ASH. Come on, Scott; let's go see what that was.

SCOTT. OK, OK … for a job like this, you gotta bring in the muscle.

SHELLY. Be careful.

ASH. Back in a minute.

(SCOTT and ASH climb down into the cellar.)

LINDA. Hey, Ash! Scotty! You find anything? Ash. Scotty. Ash! Scott!

SHELLY. They're just kidding around … aren't they?

CHERYL. Guys, stop screwing around. Are you OK? Say something.

LINDA. Ash!

SHELLY. Scotty?

(SCOTT jumps up and scares everyone.)

SCOTT. BOO!! Ha ha ha, you dumb idiots. OMG, what a bunch of pansies.

ASH. Look at all the cool stuff we found. Help me up with it.

SCOTT *(taking items from ASH)*. Check it out. An axe, a gun.

ASH. I bet it still shoots.

SCOTT. Probably does.

(SHELLY holds the barrel up to her face. SCOTT pulls it away.)

SCOTT *(cont'd)*. Hey do you guys sell these at S-Mart? *(Holds up a dagger.)*

ASH. Ancient daggers? No.

LINDA. What else you got there, Ash?

ASH. Oh God. Look at this book.

(ASH holds up the Necronomicon.)

LINDA. Creepy.

SHELLY. Super creepy!

ASH. It's not even in English.

CHERYL. Guys, we shouldn't be going through this stuff. It's not ours.

SCOTT *(mockingly)*. We shouldn't be going through this stuff. It's not ours. Shut your pie hole, Cheryl! You're always ruining our fun. Hey look—a tape recorder. OK, shhhh … let's see what's on it. *(Plays the tape recorder.)*

KNOWBY *(on tape)*. This is Professor Raymond Knowby, Department of Ancient History, log entry number two. I believe I have made a significant find in the Castle of Candar, having journeyed there with my daughter Annie and Associate Professor Ed Getly. It was in the rear chamber of the castle that we stumbled upon something remarkable; Necronomicon Ex Mortis, roughly translated, the "Book of the Dead." The book is bound in human flesh and inked in human blood. I brought the book to this cabin where I could study it undisturbed. It was here that I began the translations. The book speaks of a spiritual presence; a thing of evil that roams the forests and the dark bowers of man's domain. It is through the recitation of the book's passages that this dark spirit is given license to possess the living. Included here are the phonetic pronunciations of those passages. Cunda astratta montose eargrets gutt nos veratoos canda amantos canda

CHERYL. Shut it off!
KNOWBY. Canda
CHERYL. Shut it off!
KNOWBY. Canda
CHERYL *(screaming)*. Shut it off!!!

(A tree smashes through the window. CHERYL screams and exits to the bedroom.)

LINDA. Cheryl, don't go! It was just the wind. Scott, how could you?

(LINDA follows CHERYL into the bedroom.)

ASH. Scott, why did you keep playing that tape? You saw it was upsetting Cheryl. You just don't know when you're taking something too far.

SCOTT. It's just a joke! I was just screwing around.

ASH. Still, you scared her half to death.

SCOTT. So the wind blew a tree through the window. Ohhhh, scary. Geez, no one around here knows how to have any fun. Come on Shelly, let's be as quiet as possible in the other room… And when I say be as quiet as possible… I don't mean we'll sit in silence… I mean we'll be making out.

SHELLY. OK, Scotty.

(SCOTT and SHELLY exit.)

Scene 3

(LINDA enters.)

ASH. Is Cheryl all right?

LINDA. Yeah, she's fine. She was just a bit freaked out by that tape.

ASH. That's my sister for you, always running scared of old audio recordings.

LINDA. Ash, I know she's been acting up a bit, but it was still very nice of you to invite your sister up this week.

ASH. Honey, you talked me into it.

LINDA. I know, but still. It was very considerate of you. You're a kind and sweet and generous person, and Cheryl's lucky to have you.

ASH. Listen; let's forget about Cheryl. We're here in this cabin. Alone. This should be time for us.

LINDA. You're right. It is pretty romantic up here.

ASH. What do you say we snuggle up and get cozy, huh baby? After all, I'm a man and you're a woman ... least last time I checked.

LINDA. OK.

ASH. I have something else for you too.

(ASH gives LINDA a jewelry box. LINDA opens it to reveal a necklace.)

ASH *(cont'd)*. So what do you think, kid?

LINDA. Oh Ash, I love it. Would you put it on?

ASH. Oh yeah, sure. I was going to give it to you before we came up here, but things got so hectic, this is really the first chance we've had to be alone.

LINDA. Oh Ash! It's beautiful. I really love it. I promise I'll never take it off for as long as I live. Who ever thought when I took that job at S-Mart that I would meet the man of my dreams?

ASH. Well, I never thought I'd fall in love with one of my co-workers either. Nothing about that in the S-Mart employee manual.

(#2: "Housewares Employee")

ASH *(cont'd)*.
>LITTLE DID I KNOW THAT DAY
>WHEN I DROPPED OFF MY RÉSUMÉ
>AT THE LOCAL S-MART STORE
>THAT ANOTHER EMPLOYEE I'D FALL FOR

LINDA.
>MY JOB WAS IN THE CHECKOUT AISLE
>S-MART SERVICE WITH A SMILE
>I HATED WORK, IT WAS A BORE
>BUT ALL THAT CHANGED WHEN YOU WALKED
>THROUGH THE DOOR

ASH.
>I WAS ASSIGNED TO AISLE THREE.

LINDA.
>AND THAT IS WHERE YOU FELL FOR ME.

ASH.
>A LOVE SO STRONG IT HAD TO BE

LINDA.
>PERFECT RETAIL …

ASH & LINDA.
>HARMONY
>I HAVE TO ASK A QUESTION TO THE GODS ABOVE.
>HOW WERE WE DEEMED WORTHY OF THIS
>   PERFECT LOVE?

ASH & LINDA *(cont'd)*.
>I'LL ASK THE TREES, I'LL ASK THE SKY
>I'LL ASK THE WHOLE WIDE WORLD

ASH.
>HOW DID A HOUSEWARES EMPLOYEE LAND THE
>PERFECT GIRL?

LINDA.
>HOW DID THE PERFECT GIRL LAND A
>   HOUSEWARES EMPLOYEE?
>I COULD BARELY FOCUS ON MY CHECKOUT LINE
>YOUR POLYESTER SHIRT ALWAYS ON MY MIND
>FANTASIES TOOK OVER ME
>I'D FORGET TO SCAN ITEMS AND GIVE 'EM FOR FREE

ASH.
>HOW COULD I CONCENTRATE ON HOUSEWARES?
>WHO CARES ABOUT BLENDERS WHEN YOU'RE
>   RIGHT THERE
>OUR ROLES REVERSED THERE IS NO DOUBT
>'CAUSE I WAS THE ONE WHO WAS CHECKING YOU
>   OUT

LINDA.
>I HAD A MAJOR CRUSH ON YOU

ASH.
>WHEN I WAS NEAR YOU MY LOVE GREW

LINDA.
>FINDING LOVE AT WORK, I'LL NEVER FORGET

ASH.
>IT'S BETTER THAN MEETING ON THE
>   BACHELORETTE

ASH & LINDA.
> I HAVE TO ASK A QUESTION TO THE GODS ABOVE.
> HOW WERE WE DEEMED WORTHY OF THIS
>   PERFECT LOVE?
> I'LL ASK THE TREES, I'LL ASK THE SKY
> I'LL ASK THE WHOLE WIDE WORLD

ASH.
> HOW DID A HOUSEWARES EMPLOYEE LAND THE
> PERFECT GIRL?

LINDA.
> HOW DID THE PERFECT GIRL LAND A
>   HOUSEWARES EMPLOYEE?

ASH.
> STOCKING THE SHELVES
> WAS ALL I THOUGHT WOULD BE
> BUT FINDING MY TRUE LOVE AT S-MART
> THAT MAKES THIS JOB SO GROOVY

ASH & LINDA.
> I HAVE TO ASK A QUESTION
> TO THE GODS ABOVE.
> HOW WERE WE DEEMED WORTHY OF THIS
>   PERFECT LOVE?
> I'LL ASK THE TREES, I'LL ASK THE SKY
> I'LL ASK THE WHOLE WIDE WORLD

ASH.
> HOW DID A HOUSEWARES EMPLOYEE LAND THE
>   PERFECT GIRL?

LINDA.
> HOW DID THE PERFECT GIRL LAND A ...

ASH & LINDA.
　　HOUSEWARES EMPLOYEE?

ASH. Gimme some sugar baby.

(ASH and LINDA kiss and exit together. CHERYL enters, passes the couple and heads towards the kitchen.)

Scene 4

EVIL FORCE *(as creepy as possible)*. Join us. Join us.

(CHERYL pops her head up from behind the counter.)

EVIL FORCE. Join us. Join us!
CHERYL. Hello?
EVIL FORCE *(in as normal a voice as possible)*. Join us.

(CHERYL knows the sound is coming from outside. She starts to head for the door, and pauses.)

CHERYL. Now Mother always said that whenever you hear a strange, frightening and potentially life-threatening ghostly chant coming from the dark woods that there's only one thing you should do … not wake the others and go investigate it alone!

(CHERYL exits.)

(#2a: "Cheryl vs. the Trees")

(Outside the cabin. CHERYL is walking through the trees [well, 3 people dressed as trees]. Every time she turns her back, the EVIL TREES move behind her.)

CHERYL *(cont'd)*. Hello? Is anybody out here? All I see are these trees.

EVIL FORCE. Join us.

CHERYL. Hello.

EVIL FORCE. Join us.

CHERYL. I heard you. I heard you before.

EVIL FORCE. Join us!

CHERYL. I know someone is out here.

EVIL FORCE. Join us!!!

(The EVIL TREES attack CHERYL. She runs away, but the EVIL TREES chase her. They attempt to grab her many times and fail. Finally the EVIL TREES grab CHERYL.

Blackout.)

Scene 5

(Inside the cabin. ASH, LINDA, SCOTT and SHELLY are eating brownies. CHERYL bangs on the door from outside.)

CHERYL *(offstage)*. Ashley! Open the door! Ashley! Ashley!

(ASH opens the door. CHERYL enters, beaten and bruised, with her clothes ripped to shreds.)

ASH. Cheryl?

SCOTT. What the heck happened to you?

ASH. Are you OK?

LINDA. What's wrong?

SHELLY. Her name's Cheryl right?

ASH. Cheryl, did something in the woods do this to you?

CHERYL. No! It was the woods themselves! They're alive, Ashley! The trees! They're alive.

LINDA. Ash, why don't I take her in the back room so she can lie down.

CHERYL. I'm not lying down! I want to get out of here. I want to leave this place right now. Right now, Ashley!

SCOTT. Wait a minute. I sure as frig ain't leaving any place tonight.

SHELLY. Cheryl.

LINDA. Cheryl.

SCOTT. Come on, Cheryl; is now really the time to be acting like a stupid jerk?

ASH. Cheryl, there's nothing out there. Trees do not attack people.

CHERYL. Ashley! Will you drive me into town or not?

ASH. What? Right now? Look, sure, sure, I'll take you into town, but just listen to what you're saying.

CHERYL. I don't care how it sounds. I wanna get out of this place right now.

ASH. OK, maybe you could stay somewhere in town tonight. Come on let's go to the car.

(SCOTT and SHELLY groan in protest.)

ASH *(cont'd)*. Don't worry everyone, I'll get her in a motel and be back in no time. Our vacation will resume as planned momentarily.

LINDA. This is very sweet of you, Ash. When you get back, I'll bake you some cookies.

ASH. Sounds like a plan. Come on, Cheryl.

(Blackout.

Outside the cabin. ASH and CHERYL are walking through the woods.)

ASH. Don't worry; you'll be in a safe hotel in no time. And maybe then you can calm down, watch TV, eat overpriced Pringles from the mini-bar, steal as many little soaps and shoe horns you can fit in your bag …

CHERYL. You believe me, don't you, Ashley? You believe that there's something out here.

ASH. Well, it doesn't matter if I believe you. I'll take you to town, and leave it at that. We just have to cross this bridge …

(The lights come up on the bridge, covered in caution tape.)

CHERYL. The bridge!

ASH. How did this happen? It's been destroyed. There's no way out of here.

(#3: "It Won't Let Us Leave")

CHERYL.
> CAN'T YOU SEE?
> WHY DON'T YOU BELIEVE?
> IT WON'T LET US LEAVE,
> IT WON'T LET US LEAVE.
>
> LISTEN TO ME
> WHY DO YOUR EYES DECEIVE?
> FINALLY BELIEVE
> IT WON'T LET US LEAVE,
> IT WON'T LET US LEAVE.

(ASH hugs CHERYL.

Blackout.)

Scene 6

(The airport.)

AIRPORT ANNOUNCER *(V.O.)*. Flight 86A, the hourly shuttle from Cairo, has just landed in Terminal One. Once again, that's Flight 86A, the hourly shuttle from Cairo. Terminal One.

(ANNIE enters carrying luggage. ED is waiting for her.)

ANNIE. Ed!

ED. Annie! How was—

ANNIE. How was my flight? Not great. *Spiderman* was the in-flight movie. And yeesh! Let's just say that was poorly directed. But let me tell you about my expedition. I found the missing pages from the Book of the Dead.

ED. What condi—

ANNIE. What condition are they in? Take a look. They haven't aged a day in over three thousand years. Maybe longer.

ED. When do—

ANNIE. When do we begin the translations? Tonight. I hope everything is all set with my father. I haven't spoken with him in a week. There's no phone in the cabin. We'll take your car; it'll take us about an hour to get there.

ED. You hinted—

ANNIE. Yes. I did hint in my telegram that my father was on to something in the first part of his translations.

ED. What—

ANNIE. What was it he found in the Book of the Dead? Probably nothing. But just possibly, a doorway to another world.

ED. There—

ANNIE. Thanks for pointing that out Ed. There does appear to be a slight tear in my sleeve.

ED. You—

ANNIE. You're right. We can fix it when we get to the cabin.

ED. I—

ANNIE. Oh, I missed you too, Ed.

ED. G—

ANNIE. No, I'm glad we finally had this chance to talk.

(ANNIE and ED exit.)

Scene 7

(Nighttime, in the cabin.

ASH is playing the tape recorder by himself in the corner. CHERYL is looking out the window with her back to the audience. LINDA is holding a board game.)

KNOWBY *(on tape)*. It's only been a few hours since I've translated and spoken aloud the first of the demon resurrection passages from the Book of the Dead. May God forgive me for what I have unleashed unto this earth. I have seen the dark shadows moving in the woods and I have no doubt that whatever I have resurrected through this book is sure to come calling … for me.

LINDA. Ash honey, why don't you stop playing around with that tape. Why don't we play a game.

ASH. In a little bit, baby.

LINDA. OK. Scott, Shelly, you guys wanna play a game?

SCOTT *(offstage)*. Coming.

(SCOTT and SHELLY enter.)

SCOTT *(cont'd)*. What are we playing?

LINDA. Let's play Guess the Word.

SHELLY. How do you play that?

LINDA. Well, I'll give you some clues and you try to guess the word.

(SHELLY looks confused. LINDA pulls out a stack of game cards.)

LINDA *(cont'd)*. OK, first word. This is easy. It's the greatest city in the world.

SCOTT. Jacksonville, Florida.

Linda. Correct. Now you, Shelly. It's big. It's green. It goes in the water.

SHELLY. Toaster.

LINDA. No. No, the word was Crocodile.

SHELLY. Crocodile! Yay!

LINDA. OK next card. It's when you're playing football and you score it's a—

SHELLY. A rouge!

CHERYL *(still with her back to the group)*. A touchdown.

LINDA. Right, Cheryl. OK when you eat lunch on a blanket in a park it's a …

CHERYL. Picnic.

LINDA. OK when I go—

CHERYL. Butcher.

LINDA. Right. OK it's a—

CHERYL. Vitamin C.

(They all look at each other strangely. LINDA goes through the cards quickly.)

CHERYL *(cont'd)*. Muscle, porridge, dental floss, quintuplets, hamster.

SCOTT. She's been studying the cards. Nobody's that good at Guess the Word.

LINDA. Cheryl, is everything OK?

(#4: " Look Who's Evil Now")

(CHERYL turns and reveals she is a demon.

NOTE: From this point on, every time someone is about to turn into a demon, the same opening sting from "Look Who's Evil Now" will play. Then they will reveal they are a demon.)

CHERYL.
WHY HAVE YOU DISTURBED OUR SLEEP?
AWAKENED US FROM OUR ANCIENT SLUMBER
YOU WILL DIE! NIGHTMARE IS BEFORE YOU.
LIKE OTHERS BEFORE YOU, YOU'RE GONNA
    TUMBLE.

ONE BY ONE
WE'RE GONNA TAKE YOU.
ONE BY ONE
NOTHING YOU CAN DO
ONE BY ONE
YOU'LL SURELY FALL
ONE BY ONE
WE'RE GONNA KILL YOU ALL.

NOW I'LL ASK YOU A QUESTION, NOT WHERE OR
    WHY OR HOW!
BUT WHO?
LOOK WHO'S EVIL NOW!

(CHERYL collapses on the floor.)

SCOTT. What the heck happened to her? I mean I've seen games of Guess the Word bring out the worst in people, but that's freaking ridiculous.

ASH. Guys, I think that when we played that tape, some evil force must have been awakened that took over Cheryl's soul and made her a demon.

SCOTT. Thanks for the update, NCIS New Orleans. I think the rest of us figured that one out already.

LINDA. Did you see her eyes? Oh Ash, I'm scared. What's wrong with her?

ASH. I'm no doctor, but she looks sick. Let's put a blanket on her.

(ASH puts the blanket on CHERYL and à la James Brown, she hops up and throws the blanket off.)

CHERYL.
WHOOAAAAAAAAA!!! SOCK IT TO ME, BABY!
LOOK WHO'S EVIL
LOOK WHO'S EVIL
LOOK WHO'S EVIL NOW

I SAID A LOOK WHO'S EVIL
LOOK WHO'S EVIL
LOOK WHO'S EVIL NOW

I HEARD YOU SUCKERS MOCKING ME AND
    CALLING ME A PRUDE
LETS SEE IF YOU'RE STILL LAUGHING WHEN I RIP
    OUT YOUR FALLOPIAN TUBES
I'LL TWIST YOUR NOSE HAIR, AND BEAT YOUR
    BROWN EYES BLUE
THEN I'LL SMASH YOUR SKULL AND MAKE A
    GOOEY BRAIN FONDUE
JUST TRY AND MESS WITH ME

> I'LL SHOW YOU WHERE YOUR GRAVE IS
> IF BEING EVIL'S COOL
> CONSIDER ME *MILES DAVIS*
> NOW I'LL ASK YOU A QUESTION, NOT WHERE OR
>   WHY OR HOW
> BUT WHO?
> LOOK WHO'S EVIL NOW!

Now I told you earlier I would take you all out one by one, and I'm not one to make false promises—

> *SO KIDS, LET'S KICK IT!*
> *FIRST ASH,*
> *YOUR FACE I'LL BASH*
> *THEN SCOTT,*
> *I'LL EAT YOUR GUTS*
> *THEN SHELLY,*
> *I'LL SLASH YOUR BELLY*
> *THEN LINDA,*
> *I'LL STICK A PENCIL IN YA!*

(CHERYL stabs LINDA in the ankle with a pencil.)

LINDA. My ankle! I can't walk.

ASH. Take her to the bedroom and make sure she's OK.

CHERYL.
> YOU CAN'T STOP ME
> YOU CAN'T STOP ME
> YOU CAN'T STOP ME NOW
>
> *I SAY* YOU CAN'T STOP ME
> YOU CAN'T STOP ME
> YOU CAN'T STOP ME NOW

(SCOTT and ASH grab CHERYL and throw her in the cellar. They lock it up with a chain, but there is enough slack so that she can still pop her head out.)

CHERYL *(cont'd)*. You didn't stop me. You didn't stop me. You just delayed me momentarily. Who's the stupid jerk now, Scotty? Who's the stupid jerk now?

(They slam the cellar door shut.)

SCOTT. This is freaking me out, Ash.

ASH. Me too, buddy. Me too. I mean my sister just turned into a demon.

SCOTT. And a pretty freakin' foul-mouthed demon as well. Are we gonna be OK, Ash?

CHERYL *(popping up)*. Dead by dawn. You'll all be dead by dawn!

(CHERYL closes cellar door.)

ASH. Uh. Yeah, Scotty. We're gonna be fine. Perfectly fine. Well, we will be fine just as long as no one else in our party turns into a demon.

SHELLY *(screams from the bedroom)*. Ahhhhhhhh!

ASH. Come on!

(SHELLY enters, a demon.)

SHELLY.
 LOOK WHO'S EVIL NOW!!!

SCOTT.
 NOT SHELLY TOO!

SHELLY.
 OH MY GOD LIKE LOOK AT ME, I'M SO EVIL YOU GUYS
 AND NOW THAT I'M A DEMON, YOU'RE ALL GONNA DIE

I'LL TEAR YOUR BODY INTO SHREDS, *WHICH*
    TRUST ME, IS THE WORST
THEN I'LL TAKE YOUR BEATING HEART, AND USE IT
    AS A PURSE
I'M SEXY
I'M CUTE
AND SO EVIL TO BOOT
WE'LL BE SO DEEP IN BLOOD, *I'LL NEED A*
    BATHING SUIT

NOW I'LL ASK YOU A QUESTION

CHERYL.
    SING IT!

SHELLY.
    NOT WHERE OR WHY OR HOW
    BUT WHO?
    LOOK WHO'S EVIL NOW!

    Now Scott, since you were so kind as to take me on this trip, I've graciously decided that you're going to be the first one I will take with me!

CHERYL. Do your thing girl!

SHELLY & CHERYL. Join us

    Join us

    Join us

    Join us

SCOTT. Dude, grab the gun! Shoot her! Shoot it!

(As SHELLY gets closer and closer to SCOTT, ASH picks up the gun.)

ASH. I can't shoot Shelly. She's a friend of ours.

SCOTT. Come on, Ash. I met that girl at a bus stop three days ago …

(ASH throws the gun to SCOTT, and SCOTT shoots SHELLY. Bang! The music abruptly stops.

Even though she was shot, the now-bleeding SHELLY just stands there, staring at the guys with a disappointed look. SCOTT shoots SHELLY again, and this time she goes flying out the cabin door.

ASH and SCOTT look at each other in complete shock.)

(#5: "What the Heck Was That?")

ASH & SCOTT.
   WHAT THE HECK WAS THAT?

SCOTT.
   YOUR SISTER HAS TURNED INTO A ZOMBIE.

ASH & SCOTT.
   WHAT THE HECK WAS THAT?

ASH.
   YOUR GIRLFRIEND WAS A DEMON TOO.

ASH & SCOTT.
   WHAT THE HECK WAS THAT?

SCOTT.
   SHE JUST RIPPED MY PRE-RIPPED ABERCROMBIE

ASH & SCOTT.
   WHAT THE HECK WAS THAT?

ASH.
   I GOT SOME SHELLY ON MY SHOE.

ASH & SCOTT.

> WHAT DARKNESS LURKS BEYOND THIS WOODEN
> SANCTUM?
> WHAT THE HECK WAS THAT?

SCOTT.

> DUDE, THESE CHICKS BEEN ZOMBIFIED!
> I CANNOT STAY HERE ANYMORE. I'M GETTING
> OUT OF HERE.

ASH.

> NO, WE CANNOT LEAVE, LINDA'S ANKLE WON'T
> MAKE IT I FEAR.

SCOTT.

> I CANNOT STAY—I KILLED MY BAE! I MUST GO
> NOW!

ASH.

> YOU CAN'T GO NOW!

SCOTT.

> *I MUST!*

ASH.

> *YOU CAN'T!*

SCOTT.

> *I MUST!*

ASH.

> *YOU CAN'T!*

SCOTT.

> DEMONS OUT FOR BLOOD—I CAN'T TAKE THIS
> ANYMORE.

ASH.   SCOTT.
 WE DON'T EVEN KNOW IF
  THERE'S A WAY BACK,
  EXCEPT FOR THAT DARN GOTTA GO!!
  BROKEN FOOTBRIDGE! RIGHT NOW!
          I'LL FIND A ROAD
          WHERE I'LL FLAG DOWN A VAN!
 JUST LISTEN TO ME.
          NO I WON'T!
 LINDA CAN'T WALK.
          IT'S TIME TO GO!
 CANNOT HIKE.
 CAN'T EVEN STAND!

SCOTT.
 THEN WE'LL LEAVE HER, THAT'S OUR BRAND
 NEW

ASH & SCOTT.
 PLAN!! WHAT THE HECK WAS THAT?

SCOTT.
 NOW I'LL PUT AN END TO THIS VACATION.

ASH & SCOTT.
 WHAT THE HECK WAS THAT?

ASH.
 SCOTT DON'T LEAVE ME ALL ALONE

ASH & SCOTT.
 NECRONOMICON. THE BOOK OF THE DEAD.

ASH.
 THE CHANT—

SCOTT.
 A CURSE—

ASH.
THE CHICKS—

SCOTT.
I'M GONE!

ASH & SCOTT.
WHAT THE HECK WAS THAT?
IT'S THE EVIL DEAD!

(SCOTT exits, slamming the door.)

Scene 8

CHERYL *(popping up).* I can't believe you let him walk out on you like that … Scott free.

ASH. Shut up, Cheryl.

CHERYL. Where's he rushing to? I guess he's Scott's to go.

ASH. Shut up!

CHERYL. That Scott sure made like a tree … and left.

ASH. Stop it.

CHERYL. I was looking forward to biting into his flesh. The commercials say Scott's is the softest tissue.

ASH. Oh come on, that's awful.

CHERYL. I'm awful? You're awful, Ash. Look what you've done. You just killed a girl. You locked your own sister in the cellar. Your girlfriend is so hurt she can't even walk. Your best friend just abandoned you. And you, Ashley. Look at you. You're going mad.

ASH. I'm not going mad. I'm not. I'm not going mad!

CHERYL. Why don't you just accept your fate and join us, Ashley. Join us!

(#6: "Join Us")

CHERYL *(cont'd).*
> DON'T YOU WANNA JOIN THE CREW?
> YOU'LL BE DEAD AND EVIL TOO
> THE COOLEST THING TO DO
> IS JOIN US
>
> YOUR LIFE SUCKS YOU KNOW,
> WORKING S-MART'S GOTTA BLOW
> DON'T BE JUST A LAZY SCHMO
> AND JOIN US
>
> YOU'LL BE DEAD WITH NO REMORSE
> AND BE STRONG LIKE A HORSE
> YOU CAN EVEN DATE A CORPSE
> IF YOU JOIN US
>
> IMAGINE ALL THE FUN
> IF TO EVIL YOU SUCCUMB
> SO JUST LAY DOWN THAT BIG GUN

(Satanically.) and join our dark army of evil Candarian Demons as we conquer this land and take over each and every soul of the living!

ASH. No. No. I'm not going to join you. Never!

CHERYL. What's the problem, Ash? Don't you want to look beautiful like me!

ASH. Beautiful like you? Please. I'd rather look like this moose!

(ASH points to the MOOSE HEAD on the wall. Then, all of the sudden, the MOOSE HEAD springs to life, and bites ASH's hand.)

MOOSE. Why thank you!!

ASH. The dead moose!

MOOSE *(laughing)*. Actually I'm a Candarian Demon Moose, and I'm here to tell you about all the fun and excitement you'll experience if you take us up on our offer and join us!

    CAN'T YOU SEE WE'LL HAVE A SCREAM
    EVIL'S FUNNER THAN IT SEEMS
    YOU'LL PLAY ON OUR SOFTBALL TEAM
    IF YOU JOIN US

(Suddenly, all of the contents of cabin; the pictures, the books, the fridge—pretty much everything on the set—comes to life and moves with the music. They move whenever the HOUSE SPIRITS have a line.)

HOUSE SPIRITS *(coming to life)*.
    JOIN US!

MOOSE.
    WE'LL ALL HAVE A BALL
    VISIT SUPER COOL DANCE HALLS
    AND SPEND SUNDAYS AT THE MALL
    IF YOU JOIN US

HOUSE SPIRITS *(coming to life)*.
    JOIN US!

CHERYL.
    YOU CAN LEARN OUR EVIL TRICKS
    EVEN WEAR SOME EVIL KICKS
    YOU'LL SCORE SOME EVIL CHICKS
    IF YOU JOIN US

MOOSE.
    BEING EVIL IS DIVINE
    YOU'LL BE DEAD BUT SO REFINED
    PARTY LIKE IT'S NINETY NINE *AND*

(Satanically.) If you join our dark forces as we enslave all mankind, chew on their tiny brains and bathe in their hot bubbling blood!!!

ASH. AAHH! All of you shut up! Especially you, Moose. Shut up!

(The music abruptly stops.)

CHERYL. Someone hasn't been watching the Discovery Channel. Everyone knows once moose get singing, they never shut up.

MOOSE. We never shut up.

ASH. That's it! I'm getting Linda, and we are getting out of this place!

(All of the doors and windows in the cabin slam shut.)

CHERYL & MOOSE.
    YOU CAN TRY AND TAKE A STAND
    BUT WE HAVE GOT YOUR HAND

ASH *(spoken)*. What are you talking about?

CHERYL & MOOSE.
    IT'S NOT QUITE WHAT WE PLANNED
    BUT NOW WE'VE GOT YOUR HAND.

ASH. Why do you keep saying that?

CHERYL & MOOSE.
    WE'VE GOT YOUR HAND,
    YES IT'S TRUE WE'VE GOT YOUR HAND,
    YES WE FIN'LY GOT YOUR HAND
    TO JOIN US

(The stuffed BEAVER on the counter springs to life.)

BEAVER. Ha ha!

ASH. What? You've got my hand to join you? No you don't, you monsters. Why do you keep saying you got my hand to join you, huh? Why do you keep saying that?

(ASH looks to his hand that was bitten by the MOOSE earlier. And much to ASH's surprise, his own hand turns evil and strangles him.)

(#6a: "Join Us - Ash Hand Fight")

CHERYL *(childishly)*. We've got your hand! We've got your hand!

ASH. You monsters! You dirty monsters! Give me back my hand! Give me back my haaaaand!!

(ASH and his hand get into an elaborate fight. The contents of the cabin start moving non-stop as ASH's own hand beats him up. After a long battle, ASH leads his hand to the kitchen where he grabs a chainsaw.)

ASH *(cont'd)*. Who's laughing now, eh? Who's laughing now?

(ASH uses his mouth to pull the cord and start the chainsaw. He takes the chainsaw to his own hand as blood gushes into his face.

Blackout.)

Scene 9

(The woods. ANNIE and ED are walking, lost. JAKE is just standing there.)

ANNIE. It should be right around here, Ed.
ED. Mayb—

ANNIE. You're right. Maybe we should ask for directions. *(To JAKE.)* Excuse me. Excuse me, strange man wandering through the woods alone. Is this the road to the Knowby cabin?

JAKE. Firstly I wasn't supposed to be wandering these woods alone. I was supposed to be with my lovely wife Bobbie Jo. But I figured what with that Cheryl girl getting attacked by the trees and all; Bobbie Jo would have appeared a bit useless and redundant.

ANNIE. What did you say?

JAKE. Nothing.

ANNIE. Well getting back on topic, is this the road to the Knowby cabin?

JAKE. That's right. And you ain't going there. *(To ED.)* You neither.

ED *(giving up without a fight)*. OK—

ANNIE. And why not?

(JAKE lights a match, which ridiculously lights the other half of the stage, revealing the destroyed bridge.)

JAKE. The bridge is out.

ED *(quitting)*. Seems—

ANNIE. Ed's right. There must be another way in. There's got to be another road or something.

JAKE. Sure as shoot ain't no road. *(To ED.)* Why the hang do you want to go up there for anyway? Huh?

ED *(about to tell him)*. Well—

ANNIE. That's none of your business.

JAKE. Hey! I just remembered. Why, yeah … that's right. There is a trail. You could follow me. But it'll cost ya.

ANNIE. How much?

JAKE. Forty-fi—Hundred buck.

ED *(makes for his wallet to gladly pay)*. Here—

ANNIE. You're right, Ed. How do we know if this guy's even reliable?

JAKE *(to ED)*. Reliable! Why you no good city-slicking, over-cologned, v-neck sweater-wearing son of a gun, with your flappin' lips and pompous-guy attitude! How do you know if I'm reliable?

(#7: "Good Old Reliable Jake")

JAKE *(cont'd)*.
    WHO'S THE WORLD'S MOST RELIABLE HUMAN
        BEING?
    WHO'S THE ONE FOLKS CALL FOR HELP WITH
        EVERYTHING?
    WHO'S THE ONE MAN YOU CAN COUNT ON WHEN
        YOUR LIFE IS AT STAKE?

    IT'S GOOD OLD RELIABLE JAKE
    WHO CAN HELP YOU WHEN YOU'VE LOST YOUR
        KEYS?
    OR WHEN YOU NEED DOUBLE BYPASS SURGERY?
    WHO CAN BE YOUR PARTNER IN A TWO-MAN LUGE?
    AND WHO CAN SNEAK A DEAD BODY OUT YER
        HOTEL ROOM?

    WHO CAN GET GUACAMOLE AT NO EXTRA CHARGE?
    AND WHO IS FUNKIER UPTOWN THAN BRUNO
        MARS?
    WHO WAS THE INSPIRATION FOR THE SHAMROCK
        SHAKE?
    IT'S GOOD OLD RELIABLE JAKE

    WHO INVENTED THE FORMULA FOR CRAZY GLUE?
    AND WHO KISSED ALL THE CHICKS ON THE VIEW?
    WHO WAS THE LAST MAN TO WALK ON THE MOON?
    AND WHO WON THEIR FOURTH OSCAR FOR
        DIRECTING PLATOON?

JAKE *(cont'd).*
>WHO'S WON EVERY BELT IN THE U.F.C.?
>PLUS WHO'S A DOCTOR *AND PLAYS ONE ON TV?*
>IT'S ALL ME CAN'T YOU SEE, I AIN'T NO FAKE
>I'M GOOD OLD RELIABLE JAKE
>*(To ANNIE.)*
>DO YOU BELIEVE I CAN GET YOU DOWN THE
>   PATH?

ANNIE.
>I BELIEVE

JAKE *(to ED).*
>AND DO YOU BELIEVE I CAN GET YOU TO THE
>   CABIN?

ANNIE *(running in front of ED).*
>I BELIEVE

JAKE.
>YOU NEED A GUIDE TO GET YOU THROUGH THEM
>   WOODS
>AND I KNOW THAT TRAIL AND I KNOWS IT GOOD.
>YOU CAN TRUST IN ME THERE'S NO MISTAKE
>I'M GOOD OLD RELIABLE JAKE
>
>YOU CAN TRUST IN ME THERE'S NO MISTAKE
>I'M GOOD OLD RELIABLE JAKE

ANNIE. Really, Ed? After all that, you still don't think he's reliable?

JAKE. Dag nabitt!!! Now you no good city slickers follow me. I'll take you to that dang cabin.

(Blackout.)

Scene 10

(We return to the cabin to find ASH duct-taping his stub. His severed hand is on the mantle.)

ASH. Hand, we've had some good times together. I never thought it would end like this.

(ASH turns away. As soon as his back is turned, the hand springs to life and runs across the countertop. ASH turns back, and the hand instantly stops moving. ASH thinks something is different but can't figure out what it is.)

ASH *(cont'd)*. Like I was saying, hand, I feel like I know you like the back of my—

(The hand gives a gesture mocking ASH ... and this time ASH sees it.)

ASH *(cont'd)*. I hate you, hand!

(ASH tries to hit the hand and instead painfully bangs his stump. The hand runs off.)

CHERYL *(popping up)*. You're tougher than I thought, Ash. Gotta hand it to you, brother.

ASH. Shut up.

CHERYL. Let's hear it for the boy. Let's give the boy a hand.

ASH. Stop it.

CHERYL. What's your favorite animal at the zoo? The handa bear?

ASH. Enough!

CHERYL. What's your favorite tiny island in Massachusetts? Hand-tucket?

ASH. Hand-tucket? That doesn't even make sense!

(ASH jumps on the cellar door, closing it. SCOTT barges in the cabin door bloodied and beaten, with his clothes ripped to shreds.)

SCOTT. Ash! Ash!

ASH. Oh my gosh!

SCOTT. Help me!

ASH. Scotty.

SCOTT. Dude, where's your hand?

ASH. Don't worry about it. Scotty! You're going to be OK. You're going to be just fine. You'll see. What happened to you?

SCOTT. Ash. It's not going to let us leave. We're all going to die here!

ASH. No, we're not going to die.

SCOTT. We're all going to die. All of us!

ASH. No, we're not going to die! We're gonna get out of here. Now, the sun will be up in a few hours or so and we can all get out of here together. You, me, Linda, Shelly. Hmm … well … not Shelly, you shot her through the door. Now listen to me, Scotty. Is there a way around the bridge? Scotty! Listen to me please for Pete's sake! Scott!! Is there a way around the bridge?

SCOTT. There's a way. A trail. But the trees, Ash. They know. Don't you see, Ash? They're alive! It won't let us leave. Ash … death is a jerk. A stupid jerk!

(SCOTT dies.)

ASH. Scotty. Scott! NOOOO!

CHERYL *(popping up)*. Ash, in all that commotion, it looks like I accidentally scratched your favorite Carly Rae Jepson album! *(Holds up the album.)*

ASH. NOOOOOOO!

(CHERYL closes cellar door)

MOOSE *(springing to life)*. And by the way, Ash. I wasn't going to mention it earlier, but your pants look like they have a pretty nasty mustard stain on them. And if I know mustard stains like I think I do, that ain't coming out.

ASH. NOOOOOOOOO! What else can go wrong today?

(#7a: "Look Who's Evil Now [Sting #1]")

(LINDA enters, a demon.)

LINDA. Look who's evil now!

ASH. NOOOOOO!

CHERYL *(popping up)*. We've got your girlfriend! We've got your girlfriend!

ASH. Shut up, will you? Shut up! *(In disbelief.)* No, not you, Linda. Linda. Linda!

(ASH shakes LINDA. It doesn't faze her. LINDA starts laughing maniacally.)

ASH *(cont'd)*. Linda, come back. Come back.

(SCOTT springs back to life and hops to his feet. A few of his guts are now sticking out of his stomach.)

SCOTT. Ash! Kill her! Kill her, dude! She's freakin' evil.

(SCOTT dies again.)

CHERYL. Kill her if you can, loverboy.

ASH. Now, forgive me, Linda. I guess I gotta do what I gotta do.

(ASH draws the gun on demon LINDA and she magically returns back to normal.)

LINDA. Please don't, Ash. I'm fine now.

(#8: "Housewares Employee" [Reprise])

LINDA *(cont'd)*.
   I HAVE TO ASK A QUESTION TO THE GODS ABOVE

ASH.
   HOW CAN THIS BE REAL?

LINDA.
   HOW WERE WE DEEMED WORTHY OF THIS
   PERFECT LOVE?

LINDA.	ASH.
I'LL ASK THE TREES. I'LL ASK THE SKY. I'LL ASK THE WHOLE WIDE WORLD	A LOVE SO TRUE AND PURE A LOVE TO LAST FOR SURE

LINDA.
   HOW DID A HOUSEWARES EMPLOYEE LAND THE
   PERFECT GIRL?

LINDA & ASH.
   HOW DID THE PERFECT GIRL LAND A
   HOUSEWARES EMPLOYEE

ASH. I love you, Linda.

LINDA. Please, Ash … please don't hurt me. You swore— you swore that we'd always be together. I love you.

ASH. No, I won't. I won't. I promise. I love you, too, Linda.

(From beneath the closed cellar door, we hear CHERYL's normal, non-demon voice.)

CHERYL. Ashley. Ashley, help me. I'm all right now, Ashley.
ASH. Cheryl?
CHERYL. Unlock this chain and let me out.
ASH. Cheryl?

(SCOTT springs back to life with even more guts hanging out of him.)

SCOTT. Don't do it dude. She's still a demon. Both of those girls are. *(Noticing his guts.)* Oh man.

(SCOTT dies again.)

ASH. Sorry, Scotty. That is still my sister down there. I'm afraid I'm going to have to ignore your dying wish and open that cellar door.

(As ASH approaches the cellar, the demon CHERYL pops up and tries to grab him but misses.)

SCOTT *(springing back to life)*. DUDE! I TOLD YOU SO! *(Looking at more guts.)* Eeek. *(Dies again.)*
CHERYL *(mockingly)*. I'm all right now, Ashley! Come unlock this chain and let me out! Ha ha ha! Idiot! *(Closes cellar door.)*
ASH. Ah you monsters! Why are you torturing me like this? Why?

(#8a: "Look Who's Evil Now [Sting #2]")

(LINDA is once again ... a demon.)

LINDA. Look who's still evil now!
ASH. Nooo!

(LINDA jumps on ASH's back, attacking him.)

LINDA. We're going to get you. We're going to get you. Not another peep. Time to go to sleep. We-ah ha ha ha ha ha ha!

(ASH drags possessed LINDA into the kitchen. A blind in the kitchen comes down so that the audience can only see the actors in silhouette. In the silhouette, LINDA is replaced by a mannequin. ASH grabs the axe and holds it up to her.)

LINDA *(cont'd)*. Your lover is mine, and now she burns in the nether world!

SCOTT *(jumps up again)*. Dude! Chop off her head. And this time really listen to me 'cause I'm really freakin' dying. *(Dies again.)*

ASH. I'm sorry, Linda, I've got to do this. I've got to chop off your head.

LINDA. We're gonna get you. We're gonna—

(ASH chops off her head. He exits the kitchen holding a mannequin version of LINDA's head in one hand, the necklace in the other.)

ASH. I gotta admit, Linda, this isn't exactly what I had planned for this weekend *(Hanging her necklace on the wall.)* I guess you won't be needing this anymore.

LINDA *(speaking from offstage, as if the head is talking)*. Not much need for a necklace when you don't have a neck.

ASH. You're still alive?

LINDA. Alive and biting!

ASH. My hand. You're biting my only good hand. Owww! I said for you to die already. Don't make me axe you again.

(ASH wrestles with the head biting his hand. Finally, he puts it on the countertop, where LINDA's real head replaces the mannequin head.)

ASH *(cont'd)*. You're going down. Chainsaw.

LINDA. Useless. It's useless.

(LINDA'S HEADLESS BODY [a large guy who looks nothing like her] runs in with the chainsaw.)

LINDA *(cont'd)*. My body will get you. My body! I always told you I had a killer body.

(The body chases ASH with the chainsaw. ASH jumps over SCOTT—the body tries to follow, but trips on SCOTT and falls to the ground.)

ASH. Now it's time to die, you old hag.

LINDA. You found me beautiful once.

ASH. Honey, you got real ugly.

(ASH shoots the body, killing it.

ASH turns his attention to LINDA's head, which is still very much alive.)

(#9: "I'm Not a Killer")

ASH *(cont'd)*.
I'M NOT A KILLER
I'M AN S-MART EMPLOYEE
AND TO KILL A CO-WORKER
IS AGAINST COMPANY POLICY

BUT YOU TRIED TO KILL ME
SO NOW I MUST SAY GOODBYE
I'M SORRY LINDA
BUT NOW YOU MUST DIE.

(ASH takes the chainsaw to her head as he sings. Blood spatters everywhere.)

ASH *(cont'd)*.
> DIE DIE DIE DIE DIE DIE DIE DIE DIE DIE DIE DIE DIE, DIE. OH, DIE.

(ANNIE, ED and JAKE enter.)

ANNIE. Daddy, I'm home.
ASH. This isn't as bad as it looks.

(Curtain.)

End of ACT I

ACT II

Scene 1

(In a scene identical to the previous one, ASH is chopping LINDA's head with the chainsaw. But unlike the end of the last act, LINDA's real head is replaced by a mannequin head and the bodies in the corner are not there anymore.)

(#10: "I'm Not a Killer" [Reprise])

ASH.
> DIE DIE DIE DIE DIE DIE DIE DIE DIE DIE DIE DIE
> DIE DIE, OH DIE

(ANNIE, ED and JAKE enter.)

ANNIE. Daddy, I'm home.

ASH. This isn't as bad as it looks.

JAKE. How in tarnation could this not be as bad as it looks?

ASH. Well sure, there's one bloody dismembered head. But at least there's not a huge pile of bodies in the corner … anymore.

ANNIE. Oh my God! Where is my father?

(ED lunges at ASH.)

ED. What did—

(ANNIE cuts him off and lunges at ASH instead.)

ANNIE. What did you do to him? Where the heck is he? Oh, and now you've ripped my shirt sleeve. *(Rips off a part of her sleeve.)* You heathen. *(To JAKE.)* Get this murderous criminal out of my father's cabin!

57

JAKE. Will do.

ASH. Wait a minute, chief. Let's talk about this.

(JAKE knocks out ASH with one punch.)

ASH *(cont'd, half unconscious)*. Wait. Please don't. The trees. Wait. Please. The trees.

ANNIE. I hope you rot out there.

(They throw ASH out the door and put a chain on it.)

ANNIE *(cont'd)*. Daddy? Daddy? Oh my god. Daddy? My father isn't here. But these are his things. Where can he be?

(ANNIE plays the tape.)

KNOWBY *(on tape)*. It's only been a few hours since I've translated and spoken aloud the first of the demon resurrection passages from the Book of the Dead.

ANNIE *(to ED)*. Shhh … Listen up. This is my father's voice.

KNOWBY *(on tape)*. Now I fear that Candarian Demons have overtaken these grounds. May God forgive me for what I have unleashed unto this earth.

ANNIE. Candarian demons?

ASH. Wahhhhhhhhhh!

(ASH slams on the window trying to get back in. Tree branches are visibly hitting him.)

JAKE. What in the Sam Hill is that?

ANNIE. Something's out there with him!

ASH. Ah! Ah! Let me in! The trees! They're alive! The trees are alive!

JAKE. The trees are alive!

ANNIE. Well of course the trees are alive Jake, they are autotrophic organisms. But this is no time for a science lesson …

(The branches keep pounding ASH in the face.)

ASH. Let me in. Help me please!

ANNIE. Let him in.

JAKE. It's a trick, I know it!

ANNIE. Let him in.

(ANNIE opens the door, ASH runs in, wrestles with the trees a bit more and shuts the door behind him.)

ASH *(out of breath).* All right, no one goes out that door tonight. Also, whatever you do, don't go near the cellar.

ED. The cella—

(ED walks over to the cellar door. CHERYL pops up and bites him. ED falls in pain. ED remains on the floor, in the corner, with no one acknowledging him, or his injury, for the remainder of the scene.

NOTE: When he falls, ED's head should be blocked, or in the wings, so he can use his time lying on the ground to transform into a demon without the audience noticing.)

CHERYL. I'll get you, Ash. We're like a one-month free offer from Netflix. Sooner or later, you'll join us!

ASH. Shut up!

CHERYL. I'm like Guy Fieri at an all you can eat fish house—I'll swallow your soul.

ASH. Shut up!

CHERYL. It'll be like you were killed by some guy whose first name happens to be Don—you'll be Dead by Dawn!!!!

ASH. That's it!

(ASH slams the cellar door shut again.)

JAKE. What in the good gewey gravy is going on around here?

ASH. It's an old tale. You've probably heard it a hundred times. Boy and his friends go on a week long vacation in the woods. Three friends turn into Candarian demons. One friend is killed by a forest of evil trees. Two demons are killed by their boyfriends respectively, while one stays in the cellar trying to kill everything in sight. Like I said, pretty standard stuff.

ANNIE. And do all these demons only speak in bad puns?

ASH. No, as far as I can tell, she's the only one who does that.

ANNIE. Yet she's the only one you let live?

ASH. Yeah—sorry about that.

ANNIE *(overly dramatic)*. The question now is … how do we stop this?

ASH. I have no idea.

JAKE. Well that's freakin' great.

ANNIE. My father would know how to stop it.

ASH. Well honey, your daddy ain't here. So the only thing we can do is stay put and ride this out till dawn.

JAKE. That's a crappy idea. I ain't staying in this crappy craphole till morning. I'm going. I'm going to get on that there trail—

ASH. Nobody's going out that door, not till daylight.

JAKE. Now you listen to me—

ASH. No, you listen to me.

JAKE. No, if one of us is going to be doing the listening …
it's you … listening to me.

ASH. No, no, no! When it comes to listening …

Scene 2

(#10a: "Look Who's Evil Now [Sting #3]")

(ED hops to his feet, a demon.)

ED. Look who's—

ANNIE. Oh my gosh—Look who's evil now!

ED. Seriously!

JAKE. Geez terwilligers! Run for your lives.

(ANNIE and JAKE scream and run for the door.)

ANNIE. Ash, run.

ASH. I don't think so.

ANNIE. You're not scared?

ASH. Not at all. You see, whenever you encounter a flock of
deadites, you have to realize there is a hierarchy about the
whole thing.

ED. Grrrrr!

ASH. Simmer down there, buddy. There's the big time
demons who pose a serious threat and then there's what I
like to call "bit part demons."

ANNIE. "Bit part demons"?

ASH. Yes, yes. Bonafide extras. Nothing special about them.
They pretty much wait around for you to kill them. They'd
never kill a guy like me … the main man … the hero, if you

will. It's just not how these stories tend to go. And that's who you are buddy, a bit part demon. So excuse me for not being scared.

CHERYL *(popping up)*. And I'm not one to agree with the living. But Ash is right. You are a bit player in this whole thing. You'd never kill a guy like him. Never. *(Closes cellar door.)*

ASH. Right. You see?

ANNIE. That's not fair. He's not a bit part demon.

ASH. Come on. He hasn't even spoken more than three words all night. We don't even know his name.

ANNIE. His name is—

ED. It's Ed!!! Well, Evil Ed now. And you don't have to defend me, Annie—they're right. They're completely right …

(#11: "Bit Part Demon")

(As the song begins, the lights come down. And right as he begins to sing, a lone spotlight illuminates on ED. But the spotlight's placement is just a bit off so that the light is barely missing ED's face.)

ED *(cont'd)*.
   I'M THAT GUY YOU SEE
   IN EVERY HORROR FLICK,

(The music stops. ED notices he is out of the light and dejectedly moves over so that he can finally be seen. The music starts up again.)

   YOU WOULDN'T REMEMBER ME
   I COME AND GO TOO QUICK.

   YOU WOULDN'T KNOW MY NAME
   I HARDLY EVER SPEAK A LINE;
   IF THE HERO KILLS A HUNDRED DEMONS,

I'D BE THE FORGETTABLE NUMBER THIRTY NINE.

'CAUSE I'M A BIT PART DEMON
A SMALL TIME MISFIT;
I SAY YOU'LL BE DEAD BY DAWN;
BUT I DON'T REALLY MEAN IT.

I'M A THREAT TO NO ONE,
THE OTHER DEADITES MAKE FUN

CHERYL.
YOU SUCK!

ED *(cont'd)*.
OF ME—
EVIL EDDY,
THE BIT PART DEMON.

ANNIE. But don't you see, Ed. We've been listening to you talk for the past two minutes. You've said a whole lot just now … just you. You're not a bit part demon anymore. You're a lead player. A star.

ED.
YOU'RE RIGHT!
NOW I SEE
THAT THIS TREND HAS BEEN DISRUPTED
I'VE SAID MORE THAN FIVE WORDS
WITHOUT BEING INTERRUPTED

I'M A BIT PART NO MORE
MY CHARACTER'S HAD A SWING
NOW IT'S TIME FOR THIS DEMON
TO SING, SING, SING

(Out of nowhere, ED grabs a top hat and cane.)
I …

(Before he can rock out—ED is shot dead by ASH. He falls on the side of the stage and remains lying there for the next four scenes.)

ASH. Now you'll have a bit part in the afterlife.

Scene 3

ANNIE. Ed! Oh Ed! Ed! *(Wailing.)* ED!

ASH. Are you still mourning over that half-wit? Get over it, woman.

ANNIE. My boyfriend just died three seconds ago.

ASH. I know. It's time to move on with your life. That's why—

ANNIE. But he was—

ASH. Hey, don't interrupt me.

ANNIE. But he—

ASH. I said don't interrupt me. Listen, baby, I'm not some preppy boy toy monkey boy you can just push around, see. I killed that guy already.

ANNIE. How can you be so heartless? So bad?

ASH. Good … bad … I'm the guy with the gun.

ANNIE. I still don't know what you're even doing here in this cabin!

ASH. I could ask you the same question.

ANNIE. It's my family's cabin.

ASH. Did I ask?

ANNIE. Are all men from Michigan such loud-mouthed braggarts?

ASH. Nope. Just me, baby … Just me.

(JAKE is ignoring this argument, staring out the window.)

JAKE. That's funny.

ASH. What?

JAKE. That trail we came in here on. It just ain't there no more. It's like the woods just swallowed her up.

ASH. How many times do I have to tell you? Those woods have a mind of their own. They're evil. That's why we can't go out there. Not till dawn.

ANNIE. Listen to him, Jake.

JAKE. What the … you mean you believe this psycho and his hoo ha jibber jabber?

ANNIE. Sure, he might have broken into my property, killed my boyfriend and possibly killed my father … but for some reason, I trust him.

JAKE *(under his breath)*. Oh for Pete's sake!

(SFX: Crickets.)

ANNIE. It's so quiet.

(SFX: Loud, crazy sounds.)

JAKE. What in the monkeyshines was that?

ASH. Maybe something trying to force its way into our world.

ANNIE. That's exactly what I think every time I hear a weird noise.

JAKE. It came from over there.

ASH. We'll all go together.

JAKE. No, no, no! You're the curious one.

(ASH heads toward the noise.)

ANNIE. Hey. I'll go with you.

(ANNIE joins ASH. JAKE follows behind, not wanting to be alone. They look around and see nothing.)

JAKE. See, I told you there weren't nothing out there no how.

(All of the sudden, the SPIRIT OF KNOWBY appears, of course this spirit is really just a guy with a flashlight under his chin.)

JAKE *(cont'd)*. Jumpin' Jehosophat. It's a ghost.

ANNIE. It's my dad.

ASH. It's a ghost dad!

ANNIE. Daddy!

KNOWBY. Annie. There is a dark spirit here that wants to destroy you. Your salvation lies there. In the pages of the book. Recite the passages. Dispel the evil. Save my soul. And your own lives!

(The SPIRIT OF KNOWBY disappears.)

Scene 4

ASH. That was weird.

ANNIE. My father … he's … he's dead.

ASH. Yeah, sure seems that way.

ANNIE. He's dead. Gone. He's … he's … I can't believe this is happening again. I just can't believe this is happening again.

ASH. What's happening again?

ANNIE. Well if you insist on prying. Lately, I've been noticing somewhat of a trend in my life, and every time I think it's about to go away, it creeps in again.

ASH. What could possibly be wrong?

ANNIE. Well, all the men in my life keep getting killed by Candarian demons.

ASH. What was that?

ANNIE. I said …

(#12: "All the Men in My Life Keep Getting Killed by Candarian Demons")

ANNIE *(cont'd)*.
ALL THE MEN IN MY LIFE
KEEP GETTING KILLED BY CANDARIAN DEMONS.

ASH.
ALL THE MEN IN YOUR LIFE KEEP GETTING KILLED
BY CANDARIAN DEMONS?

ANNIE.
FIRST THERE WAS ED
A REALLY NICE GUY
DIDN'T TALK TOO MUCH
BUT I DIDN'T MIND

I WAS ALL SET
TO MARRY HIM
BUT BEFORE WE COULD EVEN KISS
ED WAS KILLED
BY A CANDARIAN DEMON

ASH & JAKE.
CANDARIAN DEMON, CANDARIAN DEMON,
CANDARIAN DEMON

ANNIE.
THEN IT WAS DADDY

ASH & JAKE.
DADDY

ANNIE.
WHO I COULD COUNT ON

ASH & JAKE.
  AH-OOO

ANNIE.
  HE LOVED TO READ THE NECRONOMICON

ASH & JAKE.
  BOOK OF THE DEAD

ANNIE.
  HE ALSO ENJOYED

ASH & JAKE.
  AH-OOO

ANNIE.
  PLAYING BOARD GAMES

ASH & JAKE.
  GOOD FAM'LY FUN

ANNIE.
  BUT HE CAN'T SINK MY BATTLESHIP NOW
  'CAUSE DAD WAS KILLED
  BY A CANDARIAN DEMON

ASH & JAKE.
  CANDARIAN DEMON, CANDARIAN DEMON,
    CANDARIAN DEMON

ANNIE.
  THEY SAY LOVE IS CRUEL,
  AND I BELIEVE THEM
  MY HEART'S ALWAYS BROH-HOHO-KEN
  'CAUSE THE MEN IN MY LIFE
  KEEP GETTING KILLED BY CANDARIAN DEMONS
  WHY?

JAKE.
> *I DON'T KNOW.*

ASH *(in a doo-wop style voice).*
> *ANNIE BABY, I KNOW IT SEEMS BAD NOW.*
> *IT ALWAYS DOES.*
> *BUT I THINK YOU'RE EXAGGERATING A TOUCH,*
> *   SUGAR BEE.*
> *I MEAN SURE YOUR FATHER AND FIANCÉ WERE*
> *   KILLED BY CANDARIAN DEMONS,*
> *BUT THAT'S ONLY TWO MEN, ISN'T IT?*
> *I MEAN THERE'S NO WAY THAT <u>ALL</u> OF THE MEN*
> *   IN YOUR LIFE COULD HAVE BEEN KILLED BY*
> *   CANDARIAN DEMONS.*

ANNIE.
> *OH NO?*
> IT WAS HIGH SCHOOL

ASH & JAKE.
> HIGH SCHOOL

ANNIE.
> SENIOR PROM

ASH & JAKE.
> *OH YEAH*

ANNIE.
> GOING WITH MY STEADY
> HOWIE BRAHM

ASH & JAKE.
> HOWIE BRAHM

ANNIE.
> A PERFECT NIGHT

ASH & JAKE.
HOWIE BRAHM?

ANNIE.
LIKE I ALWAYS DREAMED

ASH & JAKE.
LITTLE GIRL'S DREAM

ANNIE.
BUT WHEN "STAIRWAY TO HEAVEN" BEGAN
HOW WAS KILLED BY

ASH & JAKE.
DANG

ANNIE.
A CANDARIAN DEMON

ASH & JAKE.
CANDARIAN DEMON, CANDARIAN DEMON,
CANDARIAN DEMON

ANNIE.
ALL MY COLLEGE BOYFRIENDS, MEN WHO HELD
MY HAND
MY MALE CO-WORKERS, AND PLATONIC GAY
FRIENDS
EVERY DATE I GO ON ENDS IN DEMON
BLOODSHED
AND NOW THAT I'VE MET YOU TWO GUYS, I
KNOW YOU'LL SOON BE DEAD

ASH & JAKE.
WHAT THE HECK?

ANNIE.
THEY SAY LOVE IS CRUEL,

ASH & JAKE.
> SCOOBY-DO-WAH

ANNIE.
> AND I BELIEVE THEM

ASH & JAKE.
> SCOOBY-DO-WAH

ANNIE.
> MY HEART'S ALWAYS BROH-HOHO-KEN
> 'CAUSE THE MEN IN MY LIFE
> AND I MEAN ALL THE MEN IN MY LIFE
> *EVERY SINGLE MAN* IN MY LIFE
> KEEPS GETTING KILLED
> BY CANDARIAN DEMONS.

JAKE.   ASH.
> CANDARIAN DEMONS   OOO-WEE-EE-OOOH

Scene 5

ANNIE. Don't you think it's a bit inappropriate to be touching me "there" right now?

ASH. Baby, I ain't touching nothing.

(ASH holds up his hand. ANNIE looks to JAKE. He holds up his hands to show her it's not him. ANNIE turns to reveal that the severed hand is grabbing her back.)

ASH *(cont'd).* Son of a—my hand again!

(ASH grabs the hand and tosses it. It appears on the ledge, waves at ASH and runs off.)

ANNIE. Eww. Gross. Who knows where that hand has been?

ASH. Well, luckily, I do know where that hand has been … but it's still pretty gross.

JAKE. That's it! I'm getting outta here. And with all this weird stuff going on, I ain't going alone; you two are coming with me.

ASH. If you're talking about going back out in those woods you can forget it. You heard the ghost. Annie's got to translate those passages.

JAKE. Cod sarnitt!

ANNIE. OK, as far as I can decipher there are two separate passages. One to manifest the evil forces in the flesh, and another to transport them through a rift in time and space.

ASH *(flirtatiously)*. It sure is lucky you not only showed up with these pages imperative for our survival, but that you also know the lost language required to translate them as well.

(With every word, ASH and ANNIE inch closer and closer to each other.)

ANNIE. Well Ash, if it's any consolation, I think we're pretty lucky you're here to shoot things for us. I guess together we make a pretty good—

(Just before ASH and ANNIE get too close … JAKE shoots the gun in the air.)

JAKE. That's right, lovebirds! I'm running the show now. And guess what? We're going to go out there in them woods and head home. And I told you I wasn't going alone.

ASH. You idiot. Those woods mutilated my sister, killed my best friend, and with your own eyes you saw them brutally attack me. Why do you keep insisting on going out there?

JAKE. I got no time for your "common sense." We're getting the heck out of here, all of us.

ANNIE. Don't you understand? With these pages, at least we have a chance.

JAKE. Bunch of mumbo jumbo nonsense. These pages don't mean squat.

(JAKE grabs the pages from ANNIE and throws them in the cellar.)

ANNIE. Now that was just stupid.

JAKE. Besides, now you city slickers ain't got no choice. Now move! Move.

ASH. Look. You're nuts.

JAKE. I said move!

ANNIE. No, you stupid fool.

JAKE. I'll blow your pretty head off. I'm your leader now.

ASH. Well hello, Mr. Fancy Pants. I got news for you, pal; you ain't leadin' but two things right now. Jack and squat … and Jack left town.

JAKE. Oh really?

(JAKE hits ASH with the butt of the gun, knocking him to the floor.)

JAKE *(cont'd)*. And the name's Jake. Not Jack. I just sang a whole freakin' song about it.

ANNIE. Now what did you do that for?

(ANNIE grabs JAKE; he shoves her away.)

ANNIE *(cont'd)*. And look, now I have another rip in my outfit.

(ANNIE rips more of her outfit off.)

JAKE. Boo hoo. Guess you and this dummy will just have to go down to Old Navy and buy yourself a new one.

(#12a: "Look Who's Evil Now [Sting #4]")

(ASH pops up, a demon.)

ASH. Look who's evil now!
JAKE. Oh geez!

(ASH grabs JAKE and drags him outside. ANNIE puts the chain on the door. ASH reaches through the door trying to grab her, but he can't break though the extremely weak door chain.)

ASH. Join us!

(ANNIE slams the door on him. The door begins to slam open, but the chain is preventing it from opening fully. It is unclear who is slamming open the door.)

ANNIE. You wont get me, Ash! You'll never get me, Ash!

(ANNIE sees the dagger, picks it up, unlocks the chain and stabs through the open door.)

ANNIE *(cont'd)*. Take that …

(JAKE walks in the door with a dagger in his stomach. As it turns out, ANNIE accidentally stabbed him.)

(#13: "Ode to an Accidental Stabbing")

JAKE.
GOSH DANG IT WOMAN
YOU FREAKIN' STABBED ME
GOSH DANG IT WOMAN
DO I LOOK LIKE A FREAKIN' ZOMBIE?

ANNIE.
> IT WAS A MISTAKE
> WHAT CAN I DO TO PROVE I AM SORRY?

JAKE.
> WELL, IN THE FUTURE I'D APPRECIATE IT IF YOU
> COULD
> *(Yelling.)*
> *NOT FRIGGIN' STAB ME!*
> GOSH DANG IT WOMAN

ANNIE.
> I DIDN'T MEAN TO HURT YOU

JAKE.
> YOU GOT ME IN THE LUNG

ANNIE.
> OR MAKE YOU BLEED

JAKE.
> GOSH DANG IT WOMAN

ANNIE.
> I'LL MAKE YOU FEEL BETTER

JAKE.
> THIS HURTS LIKE A SON OF A GUN

ANNIE.
> WOULD YOU LIKE SOME PEPCID A.C.?

JAKE.
> WOMAN LOOK WHAT YOU'VE DONE
> I'M BLEEDING ALL OVER THE FREAKIN' ROOM

ANNIE.
>THEN TAKE THIS CLOTH
>*(Ripping off a big piece of her clothing.)*
>AND APPLY PRESSURE TO YOUR WOUND

JAKE.
>*JUST GET ME SOMEWHERE SAFE*
>*THAT THING'S STILL OUT THERE IN THEM TREES*

ANNIE.
>NO ONE CAN HURT YOU HERE

(ANNIE leads JAKE to the other side of the cabin, and puts him down right beside the cellar door.)

CHERYL *(popping out of cellar)*.
>*WELL,* NO ONE BUT ME!
>*COME HERE, JAKEY!*

JAKE.
>GOSH DANG IT WOMAN

(JAKE is dragged into the cellar. The cellar door slams for the big finish of this number.)

ANNIE. Jake …

(The cellar door flies open, and blood shoots out of it, completely covering ANNIE. The cellar slams shut again.

Demon ASH bursts back into the cabin.)

ANNIE *(cont'd)*. Please Ash—no! Please. No.

(ASH stalks towards ANNIE, but before he can get to her, a very small spotlight illuminates on LINDA's necklace on the wall. ASH is drawn to it.)

(#13a: "Housewares Employee" [Piano Reprise])

(ASH returns to his original human state.)

ASH *(weeping)*. Oh, Linda!

(ANNIE picks up the axe and swings it at ASH, barely missing.)

ASH *(cont'd)*. No! No wait! Listen to me! I'm all right now. That thing is gone!

(She swings again, barely missing. ASH grabs the axe from her.)

ASH *(cont'd)*. Stop it! I said I was all right! Are you listening to me? Do you hear what I'm saying? I'm all right! I'm all right. Seeing my girlfriend's necklace made me all right.

ANNIE. But your girlfriend wore that necklace and she was still a Candarian demon.

ASH. I know, it seems a touch inconsistent. But trust me. I'm all right.

ANNIE. OK, maybe you are. But for how long? If we're going to beat this thing, we need those pages.

Scene 6

(The cellar swings open. CHERYL pops up ... holding the pages.)

CHERYL. These pages? You need these pages? I'll kill you before you ever get your hands on them. I'll kill you, Ash. I'll kill you.

ASH. Cheryl. I'm getting sick of you trying to kill me. *(Picks up the gun.)* See this? This is my boomstick! It's a twelve-gauge double-barreled Remington, S-Mart's top-of-the-line. You can find this in the sporting goods department. That's right—this sweet baby was made in Grand Rapids Michigan. Retails for about a hundred and nine, ninety-five. It's got a walnut stock, cobalt blue steel and a hair trigger. That's right. Shop smart. Shop S-mart. Ya got that?!

CHERYL. I'll swallow your soul.

ASH. Swallow this.

(ASH shoots CHERYL and she crumbles. But CHERYL's hand, still clutching the pages, remains sticking out of the cellar.)

(#13b: "Grabbing the Pages Fanfare)

(ASH pulls the pages from her hand, kicks her lifeless body into the cellar and slams the cellar door shut.)

Scene 7

(ANNIE tries to run to him, but as she tries to move, her skirt gets stuck in the door.)

ANNIE. My skirt is stuck. Oh screw it.

(She forces herself through; ripping a ridiculous portion of her clothing and miraculously leaving her in a perfectly-cut, very-revealing outfit.

They go in for the kiss … but ANNIE hesitates.)

ANNIE *(cont'd)*. Are you sure this appropriate? I mean my boyfriend just died twenty minutes ago. And your girlfriend died only about ten minutes before that.

ASH. We can't grieve forever.

ANNIE. You're right.

(They go in for a kiss, but again, ANNIE pulls back.)

ANNIE *(cont'd)*. Ash, wait. I think it's time we read the passages from the pages I found.

ASH. Of course.

(ASH pulls back from ANNIE and tries to shake off his attraction to her.)

ASH *(cont'd)*. Dispel this evil once and for all.

ANNIE. OK, there are two separate passages. Recitation of the first passage will make the dark spirit manifest itself in the flesh.

ASH. Why in the world would we want to do that?

ANNIE. Because we have to. But be warned, once awakened the evil will conduct a ceremonial war ritual to honor the Necronomicon.

ASH. A ceremonial war ritual honoring evil … not looking forward to that. That's going to be pretty evil … guaranteed.

ANNIE. After the ritual is complete, recitation of the second passage will create a kind of rift in time and space that we will try and force the evil back through. But Ash, if anything happens to go awry during the reading of these passages, we have to be prepared … That's why you'll need this.

(ANNIE hands him the chainsaw. He attaches it to his stump.)

(#13c: "Chainsaw Fanfare")

ASH. Groovy!

ANNIE. OK … here goes. "Nos veratos alamemnon conda."

(The cabin becomes dark as all of the previous characters return in their demon form, including SCOTT, who is not only now evil, but somehow the leader of the DEMONS as well.)

SCOTT. Conda … Conda …

(#14: "Do the Necronomicon")

CHERYL.
   NOW WE HONOR THE NECRONOMICON

CHERYL & LINDA.
   NOW WE HONOR THE NECRONOMICON

CHERYL, LINDA & ED.
   NOW WE HONOR THE NECRONOMICON

CHERYL, LINDA, ED & JAKE.
   NOW WE HONOR THE NECRONOMICON

SCOTT.
   NOW WE HONOR THE NECRONOMICON WITH OUR
     VERY OWN SPECIAL DANCE

ASH. How the heck do demons do their very own special dance?

SCOTT.
   DOWN THERE WE DANCE OUR OWN SPECIAL WAY
   LETS SHOW 'EM HOW WE DANCE WHILE OUR
     BODIES DECAY

LINDA.
   DO WE BOUNCE LIKE BACKSTREET?

SCOTT.
NOT WITHOUT A HEARTBEAT

JAKE.
DO WE SWAY LIKE ONE DIRECTION?

SCOTT.
NO THAT WOULD WASTE OUR RESURRECTION

CHERYL.
DO WE TWERK LIKE MILEY?

SCOTT.
I WOULD DOUBT THAT HIGHLY

ED.
LET'S GANGNAM STYLE LIKE THAT GUY DID

SCOTT.
NO—THAT'S JUST STUPID

DEMONS.
DEADITES ALWAYS LIKE TO GET THEIR FREAK
    ON
AND WHEN WE GET TOGETHER WE DO THE
    NECRONOMICON
DO THE NECRONOMICON
DO THE NECRONOMICON
COME ON COME ON AND DO THE
    NECRONOMICON

SCOTT.
*YOU GOTTA FOLLOW THE MOVES RIGHT TO THE
    LETTER*
IT'S JUST LIKE THE TIME WARP
ONLY BETTER

DEMONS.
> FIRST WE JUMP
> THEN WE SINK DOWN
> THEN WE GET BACK UP
> AND LASSO ALL AROUND
>
> THEN WE SPIN
> CLAP OUR HANDS
> AND TAKE A BRIEF MOMENT
> TO ACKNOWLEDGE THE BAND
>
> DO THE ROBOT
> AND THE SPRINKLER
> AND FINISH IT OFF WITH
> OUR BEST HENRY WINKLER (*AAAY*)
>
> DEADITES ALWAYS LIKE TO GET THEIR FREAK ON
> AND WHEN WE GET TOGETHER WE DO THE
>   NECRONOMICON
> DO THE NECRONOMICON
> DO THE NECRONOMICON
> COME ON COME ON AND DO THE
>   NECRONOMICON

LINDA.
> *CAN WE KILL THESE SUCKAS YET?*

SCOTT.
> *JUST WAIT A LITTLE BIT*

JAKE.
> *CAN WE BEAT 'EM WITH A SHOE?*

SCOTT.
> *NOT TILL WE'RE DONE THE TUNE*

CHERYL.
> *CAN WE MUTILATE THESE FOOLS?*

SCOTT.
>*NO, FOLLOW THE RULES*

ED.
>*CAN WE BREAK THEIR THUMBS?*

SCOTT.
>*COME ON—THAT'S JUST DUMB!*
>*AFTER OUR DANCE WE'LL ATTACK OUR OLD FRIENDS*
>*BUT BEFORE WE DO THAT LET'S NECRONOMICON*
>>*AGAIN*

DEMONS.
>FIRST WE JUMP
>THEN WE SINK DOWN
>THEN WE GET BACK UP
>AND LASSO ALL AROUND
>
>THEN WE SPIN
>CLAP OUR HANDS
>AND TAKE A BRIEF MOMENT
>TO ACKNOWLEDGE THE BAND
>
>DO THE ROBOT
>AND THE SPRINKLER
>AND FINISH IT OFF WITH
>OUR BEST HENRY WINKLER (*AAAY*)
>
>DEADITES ALWAYS LIKE TO GET THEIR FREAK ON
>AND WHEN WE GET TOGETHER WE DO THE
>>NECRONOMICON
>DO THE NECRONOMICON
>DO THE NECRONOMICON
>DO THE NECRONOMICON
>DO THE NECRONOMICON

(Dance break.)

DEMONS *(cont'd).*
>DEADITES ALWAYS LIKE TO GET THEIR FREAK ON
>AND WHEN WE GET TOGETHER WE DO THE
>>NECRONOMICON
>DO THE NECRONOMICON
>DO THE NECRONOMICON

ASH. How do we stop this horrible dance? I can't take another bad Henry Winkler impersonation. *(To DEMONS.)* That's your BEST Henry Winkler?

ANNIE. I only completed the first of the passages and that was to make the evil a thing of the flesh! They're dancing now, but soon they'll attack and take over all of mankind.

ASH. Then finish it! Quick!

ANNIE. There's still the second passage. The one to open the rift and send the evil back!

ASH. Well start reciting it! Now! Finish the passages! Get rid of it!

ANNIE. Conda nostrat—AHHHHHHH!

(The severed hand stabs ANNIE with the dagger.)

ASH. No!!! My hand again. Curse you, hand!

ANNIE. I'm dying, Ash.

ASH. No Annie, don't die. I can't destroy this evil without you.

ANNIE. You can, Ash. You can. It's time for you to stand on your own. It's time for you to fight. It's time …

(ANNIE dies in his arms.)

(#15: "It's Time")

ASH.
>*IT'S TIME,*
>TO FULFILL MY PURPOSE

ASH *(cont'd).*
> *IN LIFE*
> *WE ARE BORN WITH A DESTINY*
>
> IT'S TIME
> TO ACCEPT MY CALLING
> *TO GO*
> *ON A RAVENOUS DEMON KILLING SPREE!*
>
> IT'S TIME TO FINALLY TAKE A STAND
> FIGHT WITH MY STUMP AND MY GOOD HAND
> STOP TALKING SMACK
> AND GO ON THE ATTACK
> IT IS TIME

SCOTT. Oh it's time, Ash, but not for what you think …

DEMONS.
> OH
> IT'S TIME FOR YOU, ASH TO DIE
> IT'S TIME FOR US, ZOMBIES TO RISE
> IT'S TIME FOR YOU TO SAY GOODBYE
> IT'S TIME FOR, OH

ALL.
> IT'S TIME

ASH.
> TIME TO HURT DEMON FEELINGS
> INSIDE
> THESE HERE WALLS, THERE CAN BE ONLY ONE
>
> IT'S TIME

DEMONS.
> TIME TO FIGHT.

ASH.
  TO INCREASE DEMON
    BLEEDING
  TONIGHT

  YOU WILL DIE
  BY THE SAW OR THE GUN
  TIME TO HARASS

  TIME TO HIT THE GAS

  TIME TO KILL DEMONS
  EN MASSE
  OH IT'S TIME
  YOU KNOW

DEMONS.
  TIME TO BRAWL
  TIME TO KILL.
  TIME TO MAUL.
  SPIKE YOU LIKE
  A FOOTBALL

  IT'S TIME TO RIP YOU TO
    TATTERS
  TIME TO MAKE YOUR BLOOD
    SPLATTER
  THROUGH THE SHED

  JOIN THE
  EVIL DEAD
  IT IS TIME

ASH.
  THAT I'M RIGHT!
  I'M NOT DYING TONIGHT, IT'S A HOLIDAY!
  WHEN I'M IN DESPAIR
  I ADJUST MY HAIR AND MAKE EVIL PAY
  AT THE EDGE OF THE NIGHT,
  THERE'S NOT A DEADITE I CAN'T HANDLE!

DEMONS.
  HANDLE!

ASH.
  WHEN DANGER STRIKES
  YOU MUST SHOW THE MIGHT OF AN OX, OR A
    BEAR, OR ANY LARGE MAMMAL!

DEMONS.
  ANY LARGE MAMMAL! *YEAH!!*

DEMONS.
  IT'S TIME FOR YOU,
  ASH TO DIE
  IT'S TIME FOR US,
  ZOMBIES TO RISE
  IT'S TIME FOR YOU
  TO SAY GOODBYE
  IT TIME FOR

ASH.

  IS THAT SO?

  I THINK NO!

  ALL RIGHT, LET'S GO!

ASH & DEMONS.
> OH, IT'S TIME!!!

(ASH goes on the attack, individually killing each of the DEMONS in a variety of methods, each bloodier than the last. There's so much blood in this fight it even shoots onto the audience.

After ASH has killed them all, he is triumphant ... until suddenly, all of the DEMONS, who ASH just killed, come back to life.)

(#16: "We Will Never Die")

ASH. What? It can't be. You're coming back to life? No. I killed you. I killed you all. You're dead.

DEMONS.
> YOU MUST REALIZE
> WE WILL NEVER DIE
> WE'RE ALREADY DEAD
>
> WE'VE DIED TWICE BEFORE
> BUT WE'RE BACK FOR MORE
> YOU CAN'T STOP THE DEAD
>
> YOU CAN'T KILL THE KILLED AND YOU CAN'T PASS
>   ON THE PASSED
> NOW WE'LL TAKE THAT CHAINSAW AND WE'LL
>   SHOVE IT UP YOUR ...

ANNIE *(springing to life)*.
> *ASH!!!!!*

(ANNIE's scream brings the music to a screeching halt.)

ASH. Annie, you've sprung back to life. Seems to be happening a lot around here lately. Finish reciting the passages, Annie. Send these demons back where they came from!

ANNIE. Conda Conda Nosperoto ... DEMONTO!!!!!

(ANNIE dies. But her reading of the passages successfully opens the rift in time and space, and all of the DEMONS get sucked through the cabin door.)

ASH. You did it, kid. You did it!!!! Annie! *(Realizing she's dead.)* Annie! Annie! No!!!!

(Blackout, as the music keeps going. The curtain drops. The lights put on a wild show to the music. Basically, this instrumental interlude covers the time needed for the costume and set change for the next scene, as the audience rocks out to this groovy guitar solo.)

Scene 8

ASH *(V.O.)*. So with her dying breath, Annie read the passages, sent the Candarian demons back to the netherworld, and together we finally put a stop to this unspeakable evil.

(The curtain opens to reveal ASH is now at S-Mart surrounded by random CUSTOMERS [the previous actors in bad wigs and mustaches].)

ASH *(cont'd)*. And that, loyal S-Mart customers, is how I saved all of mankind.

CUSTOMER 1. And after saving all of mankind you came directly to work here at S-Mart?

ASH. No, I didn't come directly to work here at S-Mart. There was a brief period where I was sent back to Medieval Times and the people worshiped me as their king ... but that's another story.

FEMALE CUSTOMER. Wait, if Annie died in the middle of reading the passages, are you sure she said all the necessary words to dispel the evil correctly?

ASH. Well maybe she didn't say every single tiny little syllable, no. But basically she said them yeah ... basically.

CUSTOMER 2. Well all I can say is ... wow ... that story ... is the biggest crock of hooey I've ever heard in my life.

(They all start cracking up.)

CUSTOMER 3. I come here to buy some carpet and rug shampoo and I gotta listen to this bunk.

CUSTOMER 1. I say we ignore this idiot and get back to our savings.

CUSTOMERS. Yeah.

(The CUSTOMERS go back to their shopping. FEMALE CUSTOMER approaches ASH.)

FEMALE CUSTOMER. You know that story about you saving the earth from demons?

ASH. Yeah?

FEMALE CUSTOMER. I ... ah ... think it's kinda cute.

ASH. Oh yeah?

(#16a: "Look Who's Evil Now [Sting #5]")

(A random customer in the background, POSSESSED WOMAN, turns around and is a demon.)

POSSESSED WOMAN. Look who's evil now!

CUSTOMER 2. Holy smokes!

(POSSESSED WOMAN goes after the CUSTOMERS. The CUSTOMERS freak out. POSSESSED WOMAN grabs the baby [a doll] from MOM CUSTOMER, and runs around with it, menacingly.)

MOM CUSTOMER. My baby!

(ASH takes a gun off the shelf, still with the price tag hanging from it, and shoots it in the air. Everyone stops dead in their tracks and looks at ASH.)

ASH. Lady, I'm afraid I'm gonna have to ask you to leave the store.

POSSESSED WOMAN. Who the heck are you?

ASH. Name's Ash … housewares.

POSSESSED WOMAN. I'll swallow your soul.

ASH. Come get some.

(ASH shoots the POSSESSED WOMAN three times, killing her, and sending her flying offstage. On the final gunshot, the baby she was holding is thrown from offstage, into the air, and ASH heroically catches it. ASH returns the baby to MOM CUSTOMER.)

ASH *(cont'd)*. So do you screwheads believe I can save you from Candarian demons now?

(At this time, the actress playing the POSSESSED WOMAN will change her wig and outfit as fast as she can. Whenever possible, she will return to the stage mid-song as a completely different [non-evil] random customer for the big final number.)

(#17: "Blew That Witch Away")

CUSTOMER 2.
    WELL WE THOUGHT THAT YOU WERE MESSIN'
    WITH US

CUSTOMER 1.
WE THOUGHT YOU WERE A *LYING TWIT*

MOM CUSTOMER.
ALL THAT JIVE ABOUT YOU KILLING DEMONS

CUSTOMER 3.
IT JUST SOUNDED LIKE SCHTICK

CUSTOMER 2.
BUT APPARENTLY YOU WEREN'T TALKING SMACK

MOM CUSTOMER.
'CAUSE WE SAW THAT EVIL CHICK

FEMALE CUSTOMER.
SHE WAS GOING TO EAT US

CUSTOMER 1.
AND SEVERELY BEAT US

CUSTOMER 2.
TILL YOU SHOT HER INTO BITS

CUSTOMER 1.
THAT'S RIGHT YOU SAVED US

CUSTOMERS.
YOU SAVED OUR LIVES

MOM CUSTOMER.
YOU SAVED ME, AND MY BABY, AND THESE
GINSU KNIVES

CUSTOMERS.
YOU SAVED US ALL

CUSTOMER 3.
    YOU'RE THE BADDEST MAMMA JAMMA IN THIS
        WHOLE STRIP MALL

CUSTOMERS.
    WE THOUGHT YOU WERE A PHONY ON SOME
        MAD TIRADE
    BUT NOW WE SEE THAT YOU'RE A HERO AND YOU
        SAVED THE DAY
    BECAUSE YOU BLEW THAT WITCH AWAY *ASH!*

ASH.
    WELL I TOLD YOU I COULD KILL THESE DEMONS
    AND NONE OF YOU BELIEVED ME

CUSTOMERS.
    NO NO NO YEAH

ASH.
    THAT'S WHY YOU'RE MERELY CUSTOMERS
    WHILE I'M THE S-MART EMPLOYEE

CUSTOMERS.
    YEAH YEAH YEAH OH YEAH

ASH.
    'CAUSE I KILL WHAT LOOKS EVEN SLIGHTLY EVIL
    WHO KNOWS WHO THE NEXT VICTIM WILL BE

CUSTOMERS.
    NOT ME

ASH.
    'CAUSE I SHOOT

CUSTOMERS.
    SHOOT

ASH.
>AND KILL

CUSTOMERS.
>KILL

ASH.
>AND SAW

CUSTOMERS.
>UNTIL

ASH.
>WE NEED A CLEANUP ON AISLE THREE

CUSTOMERS.
>YOU ARE THE MAN

ASH.
>I BEAT DOWN EVIL WITH MY ONE GOOD HAND

CUSTOMERS.
>YOU'RE OUR HERO

ASH.
>I SLAP 'ROUND DEADITES LIKE THEY OWE ME
>DOUGH
>I SAW THAT DEMON TRYING TO RUIN YOUR
>SHOPPING DAY

CUSTOMERS.
>SHOPPING DAY

ASH.
>SO I GRABBED MY TWELVE GAUGE AND I BLEW
>HER AWAY

CUSTOMERS.
>BLEW THAT WITCH AWAY

CUSTOMER 1.
THAT'S RIGHT YOU BLEW

CUSTOMERS.
BLEW THAT WITCH AWAY

CUSTOMER 1.
YOU BLEW THAT WITCH AWAY

CUSTOMERS.
BLEW THAT WITCH AWAY

CUSTOMER 1.
YOU BLEW HER TO SMITHEREENS

CUSTOMERS.
BLEW THAT WITCH AWAY

CUSTOMER 1.
YOU EVEN BLEW UP HER SPLEEN

CUSTOMERS.
BLEW THAT WITCH AWAY

CUSTOMERS & CUSTOMER 1.
BLEW THAT WITCH AWAY

CUSTOMERS.
WE USED TO FREAKIN' HATE YOU AND YOUR
LYING WAYS

MOM CUSTOMER.
LYING WAYS

CUSTOMERS.
BUT NOW WE'VE CHANGED OUR MINDS AND THINK

CUSTOMERS & MOM CUSTOMER.
YOU'RE OK

MOM CUSTOMER.
YEAH

(As everyone sings, ASH rips off his S-Mart uniform revealing the outfit he has been wearing all show. He puts the chainsaw on his stub.)

CUSTOMERS.
BECAUSE YOU BLEW THAT WITCH AWAY

MOM CUSTOMER.
BLEW THAT WITCH
YOU BLEW THAT WITCH AWAY
YEAH!

CUSTOMERS.
BLEW THAT WITCH AWAY

CUSTOMERS & MOM CUSTOMER.
YEAH!

(ASH grabs FEMALE CUSTOMER and passionately kisses her as the lights go down.)

The End

(#17a: "Bows")

ALL.
CABIN IN THE WOODS OOOOH
CABIN IN THE WOODS YEAH
WE'RE *_____* RANDOM PEOPLE ON OUR WAY
    FROM AN OLD ABANDONED CABIN IN THE
    WOODS (*OH YEAH*)

(*NOTE: Please insert the number of actors on the stage for the bow.)

(#17b: "Exit Music" [aka "Groovy"])

AUTHOR'S NOTE

This high-school version of *Evil Dead The Musical* is designed to remove all references that could possibly be found offensive from the original version. But should the director desire, any line from the original may be substituted into this version as long as the director feels their audience can handle it.

Should the director desire, the author has also given permission to replace the following:

Page 38-41: "What the **Heck** Was That?" with "What the **'F'** Was That?"

Page 64: "Now you'll have a bit part in **the afterlife**" with "Now you'll have a bit part in **hell**"

Page 91: "WE THOUGHT YOU WERE A LYING **TWIT**" with "WE THOUGHT YOU WERE A LYING **PRICK**"

CASTING NOTE

As the cast for *Evil Dead The Musical* can range from eight performers to an unlimited number of performers, here are some tips on how to reduce or expand the cast to your specific needs:

Reducing the Cast Size

To use a smaller cast, roles can be doubled as described below. Smaller casts always use one actor as a FAKE SHEMP, this role is one person playing many of the non-leading roles in the show. The following is how the roles were divided off-Broadway:

SHELLY (played by ANNIE)
MOOSE (played by ED)
KNOWBY (played by FAKE SHEMP)
CUSTOMER 1 (played by JAKE)
CUSTOMER 2 (played by SCOTT)
CUSTOMER 3 (played by ED)
MOM CUSTOMER (played by CHERYL)
FEMALE CUSTOMER (played by LINDA)
POSSESSED WOMAN (played by ANNIE)
AIRPORT ANNOUNCER (played by FAKE SHEMP)
LINDA'S HEADLESS BODY (played by FAKE SHEMP)
EVIL FORCE (played by FAKE SHEMP)
SEVERED HAND (played by FAKE SHEMP)
BEAVER (a puppet played by SCOTT)
EVIL TREES (played by ED, JAKE and FAKE SHEMP)

Expanding the Chorus

Evil Dead The Musical can also be performed by as large a cast as the director desires. Here are some hints on how to expand the chorus:

EVIL TREES: There can be as many Evil Trees as desired. But there should always be a minimum of three.

HOUSE SPIRITS: These are the offstage voices who sing along to "Join Us." This is best with as many voices as possible. Traditionally, the full cast sings while simultaneously controlling the puppets that make up the moving contents of the cabin. This can be expanded however the director sees fit.

DEMONS: For "Do the Necronomicon" and "It's Time," there can be as many additional singers/dancers as the director wishes.

CUSTOMERS IN S-MART: There can be as many Customers as the director wishes. Plus, any of the lines can be performed by any lead actor or chorus member. Apart from Female Customer and Possessed Woman, the individual lines in this scene for the Customers can also be split up however the director sees fit, even for the lines in the song. Alternatively, if the director wishes that the leads take the speaking roles of Customers, the original off-Broadway casting is listed above in the "Reducing the Cast Size" section.

Optional Staging Ideas (to expand the chorus)

Based on the premiere production at Stagedoor Manor, the following are optional ideas. They are one director's vision, and these characters are not represented in the script or score:

HOWIE BRAHM: All of Annie's "men" in "All the Men in My Life Keep Getting Killed by Candarian Demons" come back to life when mentioned, and join Ash and Jake on the backup singing. This included Ed, Professor Knowby and Howie Brahm (a previously unseen character in his tuxedo from the prom). These "ghosts" even took some of Annie's lines in the song.

WOODLAND CREATURES: Numerous chorus members can dress up as animals to be a part of the opening number "Cabin in the Woods" and join in singing the chorus.

SETTING AND STAGING

Below, we outline the major set requirements necessary for production-specific elements of the original design. Feel free to create your own design, but here are our tricks in case you need the help.

The Necronomicon

The book of the dead is an important iconic image from the film. The large book of the dead has traditionally been used during the opening of the show. It is close to 3 feet tall and 2 feet wide. The cover is rigged so it can open to reveal a blank page. We then used a projection to show that page getting drawn before your eyes. The page depicts the evil passages inside.

The Cabin

The fantastic thing about the cabin is that it's a character all to itself. Every piece of the cabin set serves a purpose. Most of the set pieces should come to life and become puppets that haunted our hero. Some pieces of the set come right out of the film and should definitely be there, while others are totally original to the musical.

Trap Door

This is where Cheryl lives and is a part of the film and the show. Whether your venue has a built-in trap door or your set is designed so that the trap is higher off the ground or possibly against a wall, the actors must be able to descend into the unit. Chains "seal" the trap door and hold Cheryl inside; these are also important images.

The Kitchenette

A bay window in the cabin reveals a kitchenette. This is a controlled area we created for various blood special effects. Against the wall is a sink and a countertop that are underneath a large window. The counter space gives us a place to put our breakable plates and glasses and any other kitchen props. Over the top of the window inside the kitchenette is a shelf, where the chainsaw resides.

In the actual wall opening that reveals the kitchenette is a large countertop. Rigged over the top of that countertop, out of sight from the audience, is a kabuki drop (that is used for the head-chopping scene shadow play at the end of ACT I).

Cabinet

In front of the kitchenette is a cabinet. This essentially is a hollow box that we use at the end of ACT I for the Linda Head chainsaw scene. A large hole is cut out of the top of the cabinet so an actor's head can appear to be resting on the table. Also on the cabinet is our beaver puppet and various books that are also puppets.

Doorway/ Hallway

A curtain is used to cover an opening considered to be a hallway that connects to the bedrooms. Above the opening is the evil moose puppet (in *Evil Dead 2*, it was a deer). There is some space on both sides of the opening. The space closer to the kitchenette has a single nail in it (to hang Linda's necklace in ACT I, Scene 11). On the other side of the hallway and in a few other areas of the set, framed pictures hang that later spin when they come to life.

The Stage Left Wall

Here we find the door to the outside. This door also has a chain lock on it, which is used in ACT II, Scene 1 when Ash is being attacked by the Evil Trees. Above the door is a Freddy Krueger glove. Sam Raimi paid some tribute to Wes Craven by including it above the door in the work shed in *Evil Dead 2*.

Beside the door (L) is a coat rack that is rigged to fall across the door to block it (ACT I, Scene 9) to prevent Ash from escaping.

In the upstage corner of the L wall is a window covered by thin white curtains. The window is used during the opening window break (ACT I, Scene 2), and it also reveals the Ghost of Prof. Knowby (ACT II, Scene 3). Underneath the window is a chest. It was hollow and had various puppets on it, including a lamp. Just beside the chest on the floor (L) was a grate used to pump in smoke during the Necronomicon Dance (ACT II, Scene 7).

The space between the grate/chest and the door was a false wall that an actor could collapse through. This special effect is used in the fight scene after "It's Time" (ACT II, Scene 7). Above the false wall is a gun rack where Shelly hangs the shotgun in ACT I, Scene 2).

The Stage Right Wall

The small wall (R) of the kitchenette features a moving fish. The wall is also rigged to shoot blood into the audience during the fight scene (ACT II, Scene 7).

On the walls inside the kitchenette we find various things.

Other Puppet and Set Suggestions

- a clock with hands that spin backwards at a great speed
- a fuse box that opens and shuts
- a *Lion King* poster ripped in half. In the film, there is a scene where you see a torn poster of *The Hills Have Eyes*—our campy way of paying tribute to music theatre, just as Raimi did to horror films
- a tennis racket that rotates against the wall (also where we hide the masks for Linda's and Ash's quick onstage turns from demon to normal)
- a globe that opens in half and sings
- you'll need to cut off somebody's head. We used shadow play with the actors behind a blind in the kitchen, seeing their silhouettes, using a mannequin head, and then throwing blood against the curtain. But again, it is up to you.

NON-CABIN SCENES

Feel free to design these scenes however you want. We built three drops that we fly or track in to get us out of the cabin:

1. Happy Trees: used for the opening ("Cabin in the Woods").
2. Spooky Trees: used for the tree attack scene and also for "Good Old Reliable Jake."
3. S-Mart: resembles a large retail department store for the finale look.

Opening Number – "Cabin in the Woods"

When the audience is filling the house, usually just the Necronomicon is visible onstage. During the black, you establish the cabin in the woods.

Car

On the opening reveal, we should see the kids in the car. It's a late '70s yellow Oldsmobile Delta Royale. Sam Raimi made it famous by having it in almost every movie that he directed. It's an *Evil Dead* staple. It's really a wooden cutout of a car. Preferably, the car should be able to split into three pieces and to be held by actors to dance with them.

The Bridge

A tiny foot bridge that really only is a few steps to cross. This bridge should be light and easily struck by pulling it off the stage. One side of the bridge is intact while the other is the "destroyed" version (ACT I, Scene 5). The joke we used on the "destroyed" bridge is that it is just two pieces of caution tape. That's it. But again, you are free to show the bridge destroyed as you see fit. This bridge represents the very large bridge that is destroyed from both *Evil Dead* and *Evil Dead 2*.

Exterior Woods Scenes

In keeping with the campy feel, all of these outdoor scenes will be played downstage with drops or whatever campy fun. A safe, happy look for the opening and a spooky, eerie tree look for the other exteriors.

Airport Scene

We typically played this scene in front of the main drape. Feel free to do the same or bring in a drop or a flat, whatever you like. Perhaps an airport sign would work. Make a campy choice.

S-Mart

We need to transform the cabin into a giant Wal-Mart type store. This scene is wide open for design ideas. We would love to fly in a large S-mart logo. The design should also include S-mart icons such as:

- a flashy blue police light (blue light special)
- a "housewares" sign
- some American banners reminiscent of the set décor in the S-Mart scene in *Army of Darkness*.